Indoor Gardening

How You Can Grow Vegetables, Herbs, Flowers, and Fruits Along with Tips for Beginners Wanting to Build a Container Garden Indoors

© Copyright 2021

The contents of this book may not be reproduced, duplicated, or transmitted without direct written permission from the author.

Under no circumstances will any legal responsibility or blame be held against the publisher for any reparation, damages, or monetary loss due to the information herein, either directly or indirectly.

Legal Notice:

You cannot amend, distribute, sell, use, quote, or paraphrase any part or the content within this book without the consent of the author.

Disclaimer Notice:

Please note the information contained within this document is for educational and entertainment purposes only. No warranties of any kind are expressed or implied. Readers acknowledge that the author is not engaging in the rendering of legal, financial, medical, or professional advice. Please consult a licensed professional before attempting any techniques outlined in this book.

By reading this document, the reader agrees that under no circumstances is the author responsible for any losses, direct or indirect, which are incurred as a result of the use of the information contained within this document, including, but not limited to, errors, omissions, or inaccuracies.

Contents

INTRODUCTION 1

CHAPTER ONE: WHY YOU SHOULD START GARDENING INDOORS..3

CHAPTER TWO: THINGS TO CONSIDER FIRST 10

    UNDERSTANDING A PLANTS GROWTH CYCLE 21

CHAPTER THREE: DESIGNS FOR SUCCESSFUL INDOOR GARDENS 28

    VERTICAL GARDEN 36

    TERRARIUMS 38

    LIVING ART GARDEN 38

    WINDOWSILL HERB GARDEN 38

    HANGING BASKETS 39

    MATCHING POTS 39

    BALCONY GARDEN 40

CHAPTER FOUR: SUPPLIES FOR INDOOR GARDENING 41

CHAPTER FIVE: BUILDING CONTAINER BEDS FOR BEGINNERS 56

    WOODEN PLANTERS 58

    METAL PLANTERS 63

    PLASTIC PLANTERS 65

CHAPTER SIX: CHOOSING VEGETABLES FOR INDOOR GARDENS 67

- Carrots 69
- Tomatoes 72
- Squash 75
- Peppers 77
- Beets 79
- Cucumbers 81
- Lettuce 84
- Onions 85
- Spinach 88
- Radishes 90

CHAPTER SEVEN: GROWING HERBS INDOORS 93

- Basil 96
- Cilantro 97
- Chives 98
- Dill 99
- Oregano 100
- Mint 101
- Parsley 102
- Sage 103
- Rosemary 104
- Thyme 105

CHAPTER EIGHT: SELECTING FLOWERS TO GROW INDOORS 107

- Calendula (edible) 108
- African Violet (non-edible) 109
- Chrysanthemums (edible) 110
- Scented Geraniums (non-edible) 110
- Begonia (non-edible) 111
- Hibiscus (edible) 112
- Bromeliad (non-edible) 113
- Chenille (non-edible) 114

CHAPTER NINE: FRUIT TREE OPTIONS FOR INDOOR GARDENS 116
Strawberries 117
Lemon 118
Figs 119
Bananas 120
Mulberry 121
CHAPTER TEN: GETTING STARTED ON YOUR INDOOR GARDEN 123
CHAPTER ELEVEN: MAINTAINING YOUR INDOOR GARDEN 128
Water 128
Fertilizer 130
Repotting 131
Pruning and Harvesting 132
Pests and Diseases 134
CONCLUSION 138
HERE'S ANOTHER BOOK BY DION ROSSER THAT YOU MIGHT LIKE 139
REFERENCES 140

Introduction

Indoor gardening is best described as the act of growing plants indoors. It is innovative because it solves many homeowners and apartment dwellers who lack natural space for gardening.

The point of indoor gardening is to create a pseudo gardening environment where you can grow flowers, herbs, vegetables, and even food. Whether you are a gardener seeking fresh produce during winter or someone who has no land to garden on, indoor gardening can be right for you.

This book covers the fundamentals of indoor gardening. From the first to the last chapter, you are offered in-depth information on indoor plants. The first chapter informs you about the compelling reasons you need to build your indoor garden now.

The subsequent chapters explain the types and systems of indoor gardening, the cost of supplies, and the essentials you need before you plant your favorite vegetables, fruits, flowers, and herbs. Then, more information is provided on the best types of indoor plants to have in your indoor gardening and the process involved in caring for and maintaining the garden.

Overall, this book offers comprehensive information on gardening, whether you are a newbie or already familiar with some aspects. By the end of the book, you will be equipped with enough knowledge to start a home garden inside your apartment.

Start reading to unravel the fundamentals of indoor gardening and indoor plants!

Chapter One: Why You Should Start Gardening Indoors

Gardening is one of the main components of homesteading. Yet, many people avoid it because of the many challenges of starting an outdoor garden. Fortunately, there is the option of growing plants indoors. You can explore this option whether you are a would-be homesteader or an established member of the self-sufficient community.

It is normal to be hesitant about indoor gardening, especially if you are a newbie. Some people are less inclined to try it because they are unaware of the benefits. Plus, they may be afraid to try something new.

But it does not matter once you realize the benefits of indoor gardening. You will be more motivated to give it a chance.

This chapter aims to convince you of the need to start an indoor garden in your home and the benefits of indoor gardening. It will also explain the health benefits of indoor plants. By its end, you should be more excited than ever to start your indoor garden.

There are many reasons why you should consider growing plants inside your home. Everyone has personal reasons to start indoor gardening. Some people start it merely for fun. Others want one because the plants spruce their homes up. However, there are more significant benefits of starting an indoor garden.

Access to fresh produce is one of the most important motivators for indoor gardening. When you have your fruit, vegetable, and herb garden, there is always access to fresh produce. Many gardeners enjoy growing crops indoors because they control the seasons that way.

To have fresh fruits year-round, you only have to plan around the seasons before starting a new crop. There is nothing like "My crops aren't ready for harvest." You can use grow lights, heaters, irrigation, humidifier, etc., whenever you want fruits out of season. These will help provide the right environment for growing fruits.

Herbs are probably the most convenient to grow. You can put them in your kitchen, right next to the window where they can get lots of sunlight, and you can access them for immediate use. What gives a more wonderful feeling than snipping a few chives to mix in with your salad?

A significant benefit of indoor gardening is that it gives you control over the weather. There is no possibility of a violent wind, cold snap, or overly hot weather distressing or killing your plants.

Of course, there are varieties of hardy plants designed to withstand tough climates. But if you plan to grow more tender species, putting them inside your home will improve their chances of thriving and surviving.

Also, growing your plants indoors allows you to customize the whole gardening environment. You can choose how close to the window the plants are, whether they have drafts or supplement natural light with grow lights.

Infestation is another unpredictable element of outdoor gardening, but you can avoid it by establishing your garden inside. Naturally, you might see a couple of mealy bugs, spider mites, scales, and other nasty pests in your indoor garden. But the possibility of an infestation is much lower than when your plants are outside.

The key to avoiding infestation is to thoroughly check for would-be pests and interlopers before bringing new plants home. You can even keep them in quarantine for a few days to ensure they are healthy and safe enough to join your indoor garden. And indoor plants are easier to monitor, meaning you can stop any infestation in its root.

Unlike outdoor plants, indoor plants are protected from mice, rabbits, neighborhood cats, deer, and other animals that enjoy sneaking into outdoor gardens to feast. So, that's an added benefit for indoor gardeners.

Indoor gardening extends your growing season. Even if you enjoy grooming and tending to your plants in open light, growing them inside first provides an advantage. For instance, it allows you to give seedlings and bulbs a head start on the season.

You can start them indoors weeks before the final frost in your region. When it's time to move them outside, simply "toughen them up" by gradually introducing them to outdoor elements. For example, you can place them in a partially shady spot on your patio.

After the regular growing season, you can bring the plants back inside and keep them growing. But remember that moving them back inside the house can shock their systems. So, once again, allow them a transition period in a sheltered spot around your home.

Air purification is another reason why you might be motivated to start an indoor garden. Plants fuel their growth by creating chemical energy through photosynthesis, a process in which water and carbon dioxide convert to glucose.

During the process, they also release oxygen; plants take in carbon dioxide and produce oxygen. That is the opposite of how humans breathe by taking in oxygen and releasing carbon dioxide.

When you grow your plants indoors, this system allows them to act as automatic air purifiers. Many indoor plants can help filter dust, germs, and airborne toxins. Some include spider plants, snake plants, English ivy, and chrysanthemums.

Nothing improves the look of a room more than a bright, blooming flower or a huge, leafy plant. A single plant alone can brighten up any space. Or you can create a brilliant display with your garden to transform the appearance of your living space.

A windowsill of blooming flowers, cactus gardens, or a delicate arrangement of herbs can add a pleasant touch to your home. The environment is just more vibrant when you share your home with living plants.

Another perk of growing plants, herbs, and food inside your home is that you can control your noise exposure. Outdoor gardens leave you with little to no control over the noise of honking cars, barking dogs, loud traffic, or lawnmowers. Loud noises like these can be disruptive and, often, dangerous to your hearing.

An indoor garden is perfect for anyone with tinnitus, a ringing, whistling, or buzzing sensation in the ears. Tinnitus can signify underlying conditions, such as an ear injury, nervous symptom disorders, or hearing loss.

If you use a hearing aid, indoor gardening may suit you better than outdoor gardening. By growing your plants inside, you can get the experience of traditional gardening in a noise-controlled environment. And that can be good for your health.

Gardening is a messy endeavor, mainly due to the use of traditional soil. Luckily, you can grow plants indoors without using soil. Through Hydro Blossom, you can stop worrying about making a mess of your home.

Another type of indoor gardening is *hydroponic gardening*; hydro means water, so hydroponic gardening grows plants through nutrient solutions dissolved in water. Thus, it eliminates the need for soil or dirt. Hydro Blossom is one such nutrient solution. However, the hydroponic method can be complex, particularly for new gardeners.

Additionally, indoor gardens are easier to start than outdoor ones. Sure, you could begin with a fancy and elaborate garden. But the truth is you need not do that unless you have a lot of space to spare.

To begin, you'll need your plants, sufficient sunlight or artificial light, and containers in which to place them. The easiest way to start is to grow herbs on your windowsill. An average herb garden requires at least six hours of sunlight each day.

They are also inexpensive to set up. Your beginning expenses are seeds and plants. You can conveniently skip out on purchasing planters or pots by recycling containers you probably have in your home; butter jars, yogurt cups, and coffee cans are the right size for planting on the windowsills.

Gardening can be a lot of work. As a gardener, you need to tend to your plants, water them, ensure they get enough sunlight, and modify their environment as required. If you have a family, you can use your indoor gardening as an opportunity to teach your kids about responsibility.

By recruiting them to help, they'll get first-hand experience caring for living things and establishing a stable routine. Also, it's a chance to teach them about sustainable living, life cycles, and plant biology. The good thing is that there are varying gardening kits designed especially for kids, making the process even more engaging for your little ones.

Conclusively, plants are good for emotional therapy. Like pets, they make for great company. Tending to an indoor garden goes far beyond that. It's all about caring for another living thing's needs, which can foster a sense of compassion.

You have probably heard that plants respond positively to talking; it's also a form of therapy. Other gardening tasks such as watering, pruning, repotting, etc., are therapeutic when done the right way.

An indoor garden can reduce symptoms of stress and depression because they evoke the feeling of companionship. According to a randomized crossover study by Min-sun Lee, Juyoung Lee, and Yoshifunmi Miyazaki, "interaction with indoor plants may reduce psychological and physiological stress by suppressing autonomic nervous system activity."

This study published in the Journal of Physiological Anthropology suggested that having plants in your immediate living space or office can make you feel calm, comfortable, and soothed.

Medical experts even prescribe gardening to improve wellbeing and mental health. It's also a way of getting exercise, helping you stay fit.

Indoor or outdoor, there are many reasons you should start gardening. It is calming, therapeutic, and enjoyable. In addition, it gives an appearance of natural beauty to your environment. But indoor gardening specifically has some extra benefits that make it even more worthwhile than outdoor gardening.

In the next chapter, we'll consider the fundamental and most important steps to creating your personal indoor garden.

Chapter Two: Things to Consider First

When planning your indoor garden, certain factors determine your success, so give them careful thought. They are things that your plants need to grow, thrive, and survive, which is why you should familiarize yourself with them before you begin.

This chapter will delve deep into these things and why they are important. You'll also learn more about a plant's growth cycle and how these factors influence growth at every stage of development.

Space

Space is the first thing to consider when planning an indoor garden. Yes, the whole point of indoor gardening is to use as little space as possible to create a beautiful green environment within your home. Still, sufficient spacing is at the center of everything. It can make or mar your endeavor.

Like all living things, plants need space to live, thrive, and reproduce. The difference is that they can't move from one place to another like humans and animals. Instead, they need to remain in one limited place to take advantage of available essentials, such as air, water, and light.

This makes them more vulnerable to deprivation. If you don't provide enough space for your plants' growth, you deprive them of essentials. Therefore, you should carefully assess your available space to determine just how ideal it is for indoor gardening.

Think about where to place your garden inside your home. You may think that your windowsill is the ideal location or decide on a sunroom. But some things will determine just how ideal these places are for an indoor grow room.

The thing about indoor gardening is that it can take up as much or as little space as you have available. It depends on how big or expansive you want your grow environment to be. With limited space, you can keep the garden within the shelves and windowsills in your home.

Whether you want a small garden or a big one, your available space determines the kinds of plants you can grow. So, you need to assess and evaluate your home before purchasing certain plants. Still, you can grow all kinds of small or large indoor plants in a tiny space, such as a table or windowsill. If you want a larger garden, you might have to set up a large table or bench.

Shelves make excellent planting areas while taking up very little space. Should you choose to plant on shelves, ensure that you provide the plants with adequate light sources. For example, you might need a grow light to provide supplementary light.

Know your indoor plants' spacing requirements because these change as they grow bigger and taller.

You also need to consider plant spacing itself. Since you will be planting individually in containers and pots, you might think that plant spacing doesn't affect anything. However, separate containers or not, you can't allow your plants to grow too close to one another. If you let that happen, those plants may not receive the required natural or supplementary light. They might even receive less air than they need for proper development, depending on their proximity.

Seedlings and cuttings can be grown near one another, but the spacing requirements will increase as they grow. Eventually, you will need to move them, thin them, or risk them dying off. *(Thinning is achieved by removing the weakest plants to create more growth room for the stronger ones.)*

With sufficient growing space created, the remaining plants can effectively use the available area for their growth. More space means more airflow, which, in turn, means more light for photosynthesis. As you will soon discover, light and airflow are crucial to plants' growth.

Light

Light is one factor to consider when planning an indoor garden since plants require photosynthesis to survive, which cannot happen without light.

Unless your environment offers sufficient light, your plants can grow tall and gaunt. Even if they produce enough energy for leaves to grow, those leaves might not expand as they should. Insufficient light will hinder the appearance of flowers and fruits.

Light is either natural or artificial. Natural light can be from a windowsill or the skylight, while artificial light comes from grow lights and lamps.

Examine the amount of light, natural and manmade available in your home. Then, consider your window direction.

> • North-facing windows receive the least amount of direct light, particularly during the winter months.

- South-facing windows receive the most amount of light. They receive sufficient light from the sun in winter but get less when the sun overheated in the summer months.

- East-facing windows get the best of the morning sun for the majority of the year. They especially receive increased light in cold weather.

- West-facing windows get the best of the afternoon and late-day sunshine.

Remember that your home's lighting condition can shift from season to season. But extraneous elements such as your choice of curtains and window blinds affect it too. It also depends on other external influences such as roof overhangs, shrubs, and trees around your environment.

Before you get any plant, evaluate the hours of natural light the space offers and the quality of that light. Then, go for plants that have matching light requirements with space. Many plants tolerate low light conditions, but that isn't an indication that they are happy.

Suppose your environment doesn't provide the required light level for the kinds of plants you wish to have in your garden. In that case, you can get supplementary light sources to encourage flowering and denser foliage.

- **Low light**: Typically, low light plants are suitable for fairly dark areas, such as a north-facing window. They require very little direct light. These plants hide beneath larger plants' branches in the normal growing environment to avoid direct light. But know that low light conditions aren't appropriate for starting seeds inside the home. Also, plants in low-light environments use less water and mature more slowly. Ensure you don't over-water them in the bid to hasten their growth.

- **Medium-light**: Plants that require medium light are suitable for east-facing windowsills or near west-facing windows. They prefer to be placed in windows that are out of direct light. To start seeds in medium light, you would need additional light sources. Like low-light plants, they don't dry out as easily, so ensure you don't over-water them.

- **High light**: Any plant with high light requirements is best placed in south-facing windows or any other brightly lit location in your home. High-light plants allow you to start seed without using artificial lighting. However, the seeds sometimes need extra light to avoid turning "leggy." Locations with high light make plants dry out faster due to the warmth. So, check your plants more frequently and water them whenever you feel the soil drying up.

In the chapter about indoor gardening supplies, you will discover more about artificial lighting, particularly how to choose the best artificial lights for your plants.

Temperature

Finding the ideal growing temperature is vital for indoor gardening and is one way to ensure bountiful harvests. The atmospheric conditions of an indoor garden can tremendously affect the quantity and quality of finished crops.

Regardless of your skills, you need to make a continuous effort to master all environmental factors that can cause a significant shift in the growth and yield of your plants.

When growers talk about atmospheric conditions, they are referring to temperature and humidity. Some people prefer to lump both together, but they are distinctively different. First, we will explain temperature, then move on to humidity.

Considering the temperature of your grow room is necessary because temperature affects a plant's ability to process light and absorb nutrients and water. It plays a vital role in photosynthesis, seed germination, and fruit/flower development. If a garden's temperature falls below the acceptable range, it becomes less efficient. Then the inefficiencies cumulate and result in lower-quality yields.

Maintaining a consistent temperature in your growing environment is not debatable. The temperature should be uniform from one end of your grow room to another. It should be the same across all areas.

To increase efficiency, determine your garden's ideal temperature range, i.e., the right temperature to maximize plant growth. This is typically crop-dependent since every plant responds to temperature differently. Generally, the ideal temperature range for plants is 65 75°F. It can sometimes vary by 10°F on either side without causing a problem.

A garden consisting of fast-growing annuals should operate at a starting range of 70 to 80°F. Most annuals prefer the higher end of this range, meaning you can use it for both the vegetative and reproductive stages. You will soon discover what both stages entail in the plant growth cycle.

Plants typically prefer warmer environments. If your grow room is cooler, then you might want to stick to vegetables and winter crops; otherwise, you would need to supplement the natural temperature of your home. The closer you get to the optimal growing temperature ranges for the plants in your garden, the better and healthier they will grow.

Plants tend to go dormant in colder months and grow during warmer periods. Still, cool weather crops might not suffer under cooler conditions, while warm weather plants might become diseased and die off.

If you put your garden in a heated room, you might not have to think about additional heating at all. You need only to choose plants that match the average temperature range of the grow room.

For instance, you can grow warm-loving crops like basil in your kitchen since it is typically warm there. Your basement, on the other hand, can be home to cooler plants like parsley.

If the grow room isn't heated, supplementary heat will be needed during a cold climate. The more windows in a room, the higher the temp on sunny days. Supplemental heat is needed on overcast days and nights, which means you will need to install natural gas heating in the grow room or use electric heat.

Before you get your plants, confirm the temperature of your growing environment with a thermometer. Assuming things can get you in trouble.

Note that soil temperature is just as important as the grow room temperature. Growers seldom discuss this since most indoor gardens utilize containers for planting. But it is something worth knowing. Soil temperature is very important to a plant's growth.

Plants, in general, don't like having cold feet. If the garden is cool and the table, shelf, or bench where you sit a plant is cold, the roots can become too cold, and that could cause the plant to struggle.

To fix the problem, you only need a Styrofoam insulation barrier under your growing containers. If the grow room is freezing, the ideal solution is to get a heat map. With hydroponic gardening, you can simply use a water heater to keep the water warm during winter. In the summer months, the growing water can get too warm. In that case, you just need to use a light-colored container for planting or make use of insulation.

Humidity

Earlier, it was mentioned that humidity is the better half of a garden's atmospheric condition. Although it is just as important as temperature, many growers, especially new ones, don't pay mind to humidity. But the good thing is it usually makes itself known.

Humidity is defined as "the amount of water vapor in the air." There is usually a massive change in humidity levels from season to season, and a lack of humidity often poses a challenge to indoor gardeners. Winter is often drier than summer for plants. In winter, you might have fireplaces, furnaces, and heat pumps to keep your home warmer. All of these make the air very dry, reducing the humidity levels in your home. Most plants need humidity higher than growers can offer in the winter months.

How do you know if the humidity in your home is too low for the plants?

- The leaf tips start turning brown
- Plants become withered
- Plants lose their leaves

And sometimes, you might already know about the humidity needed by the plants in your garden, and they are not receiving it.

To increase humidity in your growing environment, use the following tips:

- Give your humidity-needing plants daily spritz to mist them. You can do this with the help of a simple hand mister.

- Increase the proximity of your plants by clustering them together. In their natural growing environment, plants grow in groups. You can recreate this in your home to increase the humidity level. The side benefit is that it also makes the environment look more decorative.

- Place your plants on trays halfway filled with water and some pebbles or rocks. Whenever the moisture evaporates, humidity levels increase. Keep the water halfway up the tray. Don't allow it to reach the tip because this would mean that the pot's bottom has to sit in water. This can cause the roots to rot. Consider slipping a saucer underneath each container. That will help: 1) prevent excess moisture from being absorbed by the plants and 2) prevent the soul from being washed into the tray when you water.

- Purchase a humidifier to use during winter. This can make a huge difference in your garden because the humidifier will help add more moisture to the air, as needed.

- One thing about indoor gardening is that anywhere can serve as a grow room, including your bathroom. Consider placing humidity-loving plants in your bathroom since this part of your home usually has more water vapor in the air. Ferns and air plants are great examples of plants that can do well in the bathroom.

Sometimes, humidity levels can become too high for your plants. High humidity levels for long periods can cause rot. Most of your plants will probably need higher humidity levels, but you must make sure you don't increase it past what they need. Otherwise, you might face problems.

Mold can develop around the plants, including the soil and leaves, when humidity is too high. So, observe your plants for mold, and if you detect none, keep the humidity at whatever level it is.

Remember that it depends on the plants you have. So, research the specific plants you are getting and cater to them according to their individual needs.

These are the four most important things to consider first when planning your very own indoor garden. However, none of these are as important as having the resources.

While indoor gardening isn't as expensive as outdoor gardening, you still need a considerable amount of money to purchase supplies and set up a garden within your home. The chapter about supplies will tell you more about the cost of starting an indoor garden from scratch.

When you talk about resources, you are also talking about time. Indoor gardening is like owning a pet. Your indoor plants demand attention and dedication from you, and you can't offer these unless you make time for it.

Before selecting the plants for your garden, ensure you think about your lifestyle. Only choose plants that require the level of dedication you are prepared to provide. If you lead a very busy life, don't choose plants that demand too much of your time.

Just as you would find a pet that matches your lifestyle, choose plants that fit in with your activity levels.

Understanding a Plants Growth Cycle

As a grower, understanding the stages of growth in plants is crucial for you. Whether you plan to get young or adult plants, familiarizing yourself with the growth cycle will teach you how to achieve maximum yield.

Many growers don't bother with the stages of growth because they think gardening is all about sticking seeds into a container and watering it until a plant appears. However, the needs of your plants change according to each stage. It's best to understand the stages, so you know what needs to meet and when. This is a basic thing every gardener should learn in the planning stage.

Seed

The seed is the origin of any plant. It contains everything a plant needs to survive until the formation of a root. A seed has three fundamental parts: the seed coat, the endosperm, and the embryo.

The seed coat is the outer part of the seed – what you see when you look at it. It is an external source of protection for the upcoming plant.

The endosperm provides everything, including nutrition, that the plant needs in its initial phase. In most seeds, it covers the embryo to serve as a source of accessible sustenance.

The third basic part of a seed is the embryo, containing the roots, cotyledon, and embryonic leaves. All of these things are carefully tucked inside a seed.

Gardener or not, everyone knows what roots are. The cotyledon serves as the external food source once the plant starts to grow. And the embryonic leaves refer to the first two leaves that appear after germination.

Since you will probably buy half-grown plants for your indoor garden, you may not witness the growth cycle at this stage. Still, it's important to be familiar with these concepts and stages; it's what caring gardeners learn.

If you start from the beginning, know that storing your seeds in a dry, airtight part of your home will obstruct them from moving on to the germination phase until the environmental conditions are just right.

Seeds can remain viable for a long time. However, the endosperm declines over time, reducing the possibility of germination.

Germination

Germination occurs when the seed finally emerges out of its shell. Before a seed can germinate, two things must be provided in abundance:

- Water: The growth process is triggered when seeds hydrate and rehydrate regularly and adequately. So, seeds need sufficient water to start germinating.

- Warmth: Heat requirements vary from plant to plant, and heat is crucial for germination. If the environment is too hot or too cold, a seed will stay dormant until the right condition is met.

Germination usually takes days to weeks, depending on what you are planting. Some trees take weeks to germinate, while most vegetables take a few days. However, certain factors can inhibit germination.

First, if you plant your seeds too deeply, they might not be able to come out of their shells. The right thing is to read and follow the instructions that come with your seeds. You shouldn't just use a random amount of soil on the plants.

Some crops prefer to be under the soil's surface, while others need to be on top of the soil. Again, you might not need to worry about this factor if you simply purchase already growing plants.

Second, seeds of poor quality won't germinate as fast as high-quality ones. Make sure the manufacturer you are buying your seeds from regularly tests for germination rates. That will ensure you aren't buying duds. Consider buying from organic and non-GMO distributors. They sell the highest quality seeds.

Third, most seeds prefer moderately moist soil to grow in. If the soil is too dry, the seeds won't sprout. And if there is too much water, the young plant may drown before it can even sprout.

When seeds first germinate, they depend on the endosperm for growth. The seed sends the root deep into the soil to form a support system that can transfer nutrients from the soil to the plant to encourage further growth.

Vegetation

Once the root has established a way for the seedling to absorb nutrients from the soil, the seed still needs to expand its leaves to acquire light and producing the energy it requires for growth.

The vegetative state is when plants grow stem, branch, and leaf areas to access light. The leaves increase and become bigger to create a larger surface area for light absorption.

During this stage, those leaves also need nitrogen for chlorophyll production. Remember that chlorophyll is the material plants need to draw in energy from the light source (s).

Reproduction

This is the phase when the plant redirects energy from growth to flowering. Energy sourced from light is now used to "go to seed." During the reproductive phase, the plant needs phosphorus because it assists with flowering and fruit growth.

You can trigger reproduction by changing the amount of daylight a plant is exposed to daily. Plants have a sensitivity to these changes, which is called photoperiodism. But they only notice the light, not its source.

And that is why you can use artificial lighting to control indoor plants' growth. As long as you provide a measure of light similar to the natural sunlight, your plants will grow indoors.

This stage is also when pollination occurs, which is when plants start developing seeds and reproducing. Since your garden will be an indoor one, you must make pollination happen yourself.

That can be easily done with a cotton swab. You gently brush against a flower's interior and move to the next flower and the next until you have successfully pollinated all your plants. The process is relatively simple and easy, and you don't need it for plants you don't plan on collecting seeds from.

Dormancy

Those who grow perennial plants are familiar with the dormant phase of the growth cycle. Perennials are those plants that live for more than one year. Many gardeners overlook this stage since they mostly grow annual plants, and those do not experience dormancy. But knowing this can be helpful if you plan to grow perennial crops.

In the dormant stage, plants hold off on growth until you provide a more suitable growing environment. It's similar to how some plants hibernate during the summer heat or the winter months. This period can make it seem like your plants are dying off. In reality, they are just conserving energy until an opportunity arises for the life cycle to continue.

Dormancy naturally occurs with seasonal changes due to lower light hours and colder weather during winter. For plants who love the cold, it often occurs during summer. The plants come back right after the heat subsides.

Indoor plants don't experience dormancy as much as outdoor ones, which is another reason to love gardening within the comfort of your home.

Consider withholding a bit of water and fertilizer during the dormant phase because the plants won't absorb as much as they do during other times of the year. On the other hand, suppose your plants start declining when you reduce their water and fertilizer application. In that case, they likely aren't in a dormant phase. So, you should keep treating them normally.

By now, you should have an informed understanding of the growth cycle and the different stages. But there is more critical information to enlighten you on your plants' needs.

Roots

Think of the root as your plants' IV. They take in nutrients, water, and air from the soil and transport these to the leaves to initiate photosynthesis, which is how your plants produce energy for growth.

If you don't create enough space for the roots to grow, the growth of your plant, tree, fruit, or flower is affected. Once the plant reaches a specific size, it may not be able to grow further.

It's like restricting your caloric intake to the number your body needs to maintain its current weight. If you don't add extra calories, you won't be able to add more weight.

But sometimes, your plant might look sickly while seemingly growing great. That might be a sign that your roots require more room to grow and absorb the necessary things to support the plant's development. You would need to re-pot the plant in that case.

On the flip side, you can run into issues concerning too much growth space for the roots. If a container is too big, that leads to "over-potting." The problem of over-potting is caused by too much soil, not the roots.

When you plant in a container larger than what you need, the water you feed the fruit or tree sits in the part of the soil where the smaller root system can't absorb nutrients, water, or air. This decreases aeration, and rather than expand, the roots begin to rot.

This problem only happens with indoor or container gardening since outdoor gardening soil drains water much better.

What happens when your plants' roots become damaged? Fortunately, most plants can regrow their roots after damage. It depends on the extent of damage caused throughout the root system. A plant eventually withers if it does not have sufficient roots to absorb energy (water, air, nutrients).

Leaves

Leaves ensure a plant's growth and continued survival by converting light to energy. To get a little technical, the photosynthesis process produces glucose to fuel the plant. One thing about leaves is that they can communicate with you. Just be a good listener. You can tell your plants' needs from the leaves' colors.

- **Yellow leaves:** If your leaves suddenly start turning yellow, it's a sign that your plants need less water or more nutrients. Stop watering your plants as often as you normally do, but still give them enough water. If the yellow doesn't go away, that could mean they need more plant food due to nutrient deficiency.

- **Yellow spots:** Indoor plants are not completely safe from pests. If your leaves start showing yellowish spots, that could signify a spider mite problem. Scale also occurs indoors, leading to other problems.

- **Brown:** Should your leaves start turning brown and crunchy, it means that your plants need more water. But ensure you don't over-water them. Just give them enough H20 to keep the soil damp. The right consistency of water will ensure that the soil keeps drying up without the leaves turning brown and crunchy.

- **No leaves:** If your plants aren't adding new leaves or the old ones aren't expanding, your plants need more sunlight or water. Without adequate water and sunlight, photosynthesis cannot happen; plants can't add new leaves or grow further. Try giving the plants more water at first. If that doesn't work, increase the light source.

Like humans, plants require certain nutrients that perform various functions, such as triggering photosynthesis or creating a solid root system. The main nutrients plants need are nitrogen, potassium, and phosphorus; every plant needs individual levels of these major nutrients to live and thrive.

Now that you are armed with a more informed understanding of plants and their needs, it's time to put your bright green thumb to work. But first, let's help you choose the best indoor garden design for your home!

Chapter Three: Designs for Successful Indoor Gardens

There are different indoor gardening approaches; each has its own design and style. One by one, we will examine these designs and how you can choose one perfectly suited for your home space and lifestyle.

When talking about indoor gardening systems, people mention vertical gardening, container or pot gardening, terrarium gardening, etc. These are all grouped into two main types of indoor gardening: soil gardening and hydroponic gardening.

Soil gardening is planting with soil, while hydroponic gardening is water-based planting. When you start setting up a green room within your house, the soil is one of the first things you get. You know that plants depend on soil for nutrients and structural stability. The healthier the soil is, the more protected plants are from pests and diseases.

Soil is much more than dirt. It offers oxygen to plants, provides the physical substrate roots need to grow, and contains a diverse community of microorganisms that fuel plants with essential nutrients like nitrogen, phosphorus, and potassium.

Hydroponics might seem like quite a strange method for growing crops to new growers and even old ones. Many lifelong growers stay away from it because it removes everything that every plant needs for growth soil away from the gardening equation.

While soil does provide the listed benefits, the fact is that it is becoming less of a necessity. Modern gardeners consider hydroponics a more convenient way of giving plants what they need from the soil: nutrients.

In hydroponic gardening, plants are grown in water-based nutrient solutions and other kinds of growing mediums without the use of soil. Indoor gardening allows you to plant with soil or hydroponics. If you wish, you can even combine both types of gardening.

Soil planting means growing your crops in containers and pots that you place in different areas across your indoor environment. Hydroponics, on the contrary, has different planting systems. Let's discuss the main hydroponic gardening systems.

- **Deepwater Culture**

This is considered the simplest hydroponics system. What separates each system of hydroponic from one another is the method of connection between plants and nutrients. In other systems, plants are separated from the nutrient solution.

In the deep-water culture system, plants are directly submerged into the nutrients reservoir. The design is simple and straightforward. First, you fill the container levels above halfway with the nutrient solution for the plants.

Then, you place the plants in a polystyrene tray designed specifically for them, which allows the plants to float on top of the water-based solution. As a result, the roots are suspended and constantly wet from the nutrient solution.

There must be an air stone bubbler or an aquarium pump in the tank to prevent root rot due to the never-ending bath. With that, your plants get to soak up nutrients without ever suffocating.

Remember that this system isn't great for all kinds of plants – even with the oxygenated air. However, it is an excellent growing environment for plants like lettuce.

To try hydroponics, the DWC system offers the right introduction, thanks to its simplicity. It is also relatively cheap to set up, making it a great idea if you are gardening on a budget.

The con is that you have to change the nutrient solution faster than any other water-based planting system. Plus, the range of plants you can use with the DWC is pretty limited.

- **Nutrient Film Technique**

This technique is somewhat extreme and complex, but growers who have tried it promise it is effective. The nutrient film technique involves placing your plants in a grow tray, the kind used in a deep-water culture system.

The tray is placed on top of the reservoir tank, which must have been filled with the nutrient solution. It is slightly tilted to place it at an angle. A pump is installed to move the nutrient solution from the tank to the grow tray, flowing over the suspended plant roots.

With the grow tray tilted, gravity makes excess nutrient solution drop back into the tank below. This reduces the amount of nutrient solution flowing over the roots while making it constant. The setup helps prevent overfeeding.

The cycle created by the nutrient pump and gravity makes sure that upkeep is necessary, no matter how small. Another crucial aspect of the NFT system is placing an air pump in the nutrient solution tank to oxygenate the water.

Plants grow faster in the NFT system, likely due to increased oxygenation, and you don't need any medium. Since it is designed to flow constantly, you need not set up a timer like other hydroponic systems.

However, this design is also more expensive than others because of the electricity and nutrient pump cost. Additionally, pumps tend to clog in the NFT system, making it somewhat high-risk.

If you don't check the system regularly and the pump clogs, that could cause your plants to starve off and croak quickly.

- **Wick System**

WICK SYSTEM

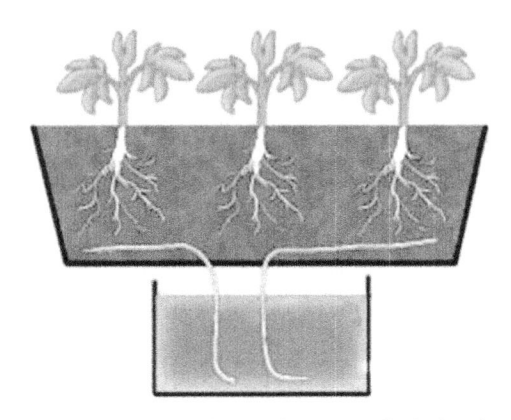

The wick system is as simple as the DWC. It is also easy to set up. In a wick system, you keep your plants in some medium, like vermiculite, which won't take too much of the nutrients. That would defeat the purpose of the medium.

There is no direct contact between the plants and the nutrient solution, which must be in its container. Instead, the plants are fed from the container through a wick. And that is why this is called the wick system.

You can use a cotton or nylon wick. The material doesn't matter, as long as it's absorbent. The best thing about the wick system is that it does not require electricity to run, making it a low-cost choice for gardeners on a budget.

The wick acts as a straw to feed the plants and you, being the grower, only have to check on them occasionally. However, it takes a relatively long time for the nutrients to transport through the wick and feed the plants.

Thus, the wick system is much more suitable for low-maintenance plants, such as herbs. It is not ideal for flowering or fruit-bearing plants due to its limited food availability.

- **Ebb & Flow**

This is one of the complicated hydroponic systems. The ebb and flow method involves putting plants in perlite, coconut coir, or vermiculite, which serves as a medium. Then arrange them in a large grow tray that goes on top of the nutrient reservoir.

Unlike the NFT, the tray isn't tilted at an angle, so you must drill holes in the bottom to make room for drainage. This system needs a timer to function efficiently. When you set up an ebb and flow system, you must also create a schedule to operate on.

The concept works by having the reservoir pump fill the tray for a fixed amount of time, long enough for the water level to reach the roots in the perlite or whatever medium you use. At that point, the pump shuts off automatically, and the solution trickles back into the tank below.

Setting a timer ensures that the process continues regularly, without underfeeding or overfeeding the plants. This system is best used for plants that have no problem being dry for some period. But you have to set the timer manually. Therefore, nothing stops you from lengthening or shortening the time interval between watering according to the crops' needs.

The only cons of the ebb and flow system are the timer and medium requirements, along with the possibility of the nutrient pump getting clogged. Other than that, it is great for airflow and the recycling of the nutrient mixture. And the timer does all the work for you.

- Aeroponics

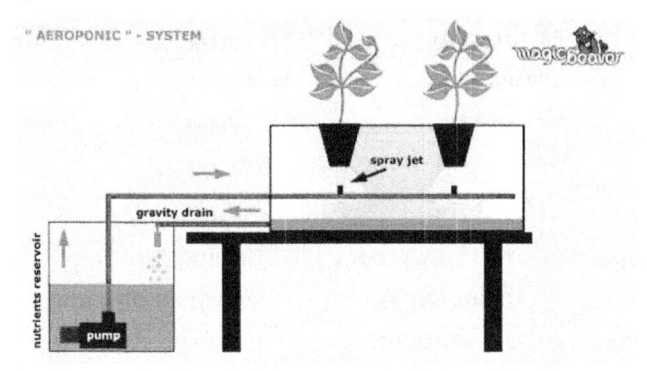

This is the most advanced and most adaptable hydroponic system. Some growers also consider it the "strangest" because of how futuristic it seems. The idea of aeroponics is to hang plants from a grow tray without using a medium, leaving the roots exposed.

Unlike all the other systems, the nutrient solution isn't dripped, transported, sucked, or poured. It's spritzed in the form of a mist. There is a water pressure built within the pump. Then, nozzles spray the solution over the plant's roots like misting your face when waiting in line around a water park.

As you can tell, this is refreshing for the plants. Compared to other systems, aeroponics use less water. Due to this, you must spray the plants as frequently as required, helped by a timer. However, thanks to the need for mist nozzles, this isn't exactly an economical choice because the nozzles are inclined to clogging.

The nutrient solution constantly recycles, and the transformation of water to mist gives the solution higher oxygen levels, leading to faster growth in some crops. Additionally, you get to control the amount and frequency of water sprayed.

These make the aeroponics system ideal for various plants, including vegetables, fruits, flowers, and herbs.

- **Drip Hydroponics**

The drip system is similar to the ebb and flow, but it is much more controlled. The grow tray containing the plants and a medium is placed on top of the nutrient tank. Rather than the medium being flooded, the nutrient solution is deposited at the plants' roots with a drip manifold and drip lines.

Like the ebb and flow technique, this system may be set up with a timer. But this isn't always necessary if the drip manifold contains emitters to regulate the speed of the water. It means you can manipulate the rate at which water gets to every individual plant in one grow tray. That alone makes drip hydroponics a versatile gardening system compared to the other systems.

Suppose you can't decide which to go for between soil and hydroponic gardening. In that case, you can make your indoor garden a blend of both, providing the best of both worlds inside your home.

Soil gardening is mostly done with containers, pots, and built-in planters. The container system is much easier than hydroponics. You can use any material you want, from plastic to metal and ceramic. Some growers even make containers from concrete. A good example is the clay pot.

Chapter eleven will explain more on the process of setting up soil or hydroponic gardening. For now, let's discuss the designs of an indoor garden.

Before you choose a design, you need to consider the space you have available because this will determine the size of your garden. But more importantly, you must consider your aesthetic value and your productivity.

How would you like your home to look when done with your garden? Would you like to make use of every available space in your home or just settle for something simple? Indoor gardening is so convenient that you can even hang plants in your bedroom if you feel like it.

Also, think about how much time you will dedicate towards setting up your grow room and maintaining it. Some garden designs are much more demanding than others. Therefore, choose a design that matches your productivity level. That will help protect your plants from possible neglect.

Different indoor gardening designs can be good for your home. However, suppose you have a small space you wish to maximize to the fullest extent. There, the vertical gardening design is the perfect choice for you.

Below are some of the best designs for a successful indoor garden. These designs take advantage of every potential grow room in a living space.

Vertical Garden

Growing crops vertically is the rave among gardeners right now, and for a good reason. Plants are placed in an upward direction aided by a support system. A vertical garden is one of the most attractive and breathtaking ways to use plants for home décor and gardening simultaneously.

It requires a bit of work to construct and set up. But once you finish, you can turn an entire wall in your home into a stunning display of greenery. Whether you want to fill up your hallway with plants or simply add a dash of nature to empty wall spaces, you can achieve your vertical garden on any desired scale.

Suppose you have little to no gardening space. In that case, indoor vertical gardening can help you utilize areas in your home otherwise unsuitable for growing crops. It is especially great for growing greens and veggies.

You can grow in containers and then place them on walls, fences, patio, balcony, or your porch. Growing vertically opens room for exponential plant growth. It saves space and is healthy for the plants.

Simply sitting your containers on the ground makes them prone to pests, rot, and diseases.

A benefit of vertical gardening is that it simplifies harvesting. For example, if you grow fruits vertically, they will simply hang from the vine, making them easier to find and pluck. There are many ways to grow crops vertically.

You can use any of these in your home or combine a few of the designs. You can utilize just about any area for growing crops, and some of the most common vertical systems for climbing plants include:

• Trellises: These are well-known plant support systems. They are used in outdoor gardens and can be used in indoor ones as well. A trellis is generally a flat structure freestanding or attached to a fence, wall, or planter. It comes in different shapes and sizes.

• Pallet container holder: This vertical gardening method can be used for growing herbs, salad greens, and ornamental plants. You just need to arrange a pallet board to hang as many containers or pots as you want. Then, you can place this on your balcony.

• Vertical planter: A vertical planter is used to stack different varieties to make a garden more attractive. You can make one by yourself or purchase it in a local or online store. It is pretty easy to make and can be set up quickly. You only need a minimum of five terracotta pots of different sizes, a variety of plants, potting soil, and a center rod to get started.

Terrariums

Terrarium gardening is achieved by creating plant worlds within a tiny glass environment. Terrariums are mini gardens, and they can be luscious and enchanting. The best thing is that you can put it in any part of your home.

However, the kinds of plants you wish to grow can influence your choice of a garden design. So, ensure you consider what to grow in your terrarium. Decide if a contained glass is the right environment for the crops you want in your garden.

Terrariums rarely have drainage holes, so remember this while choosing the right plants for you. Keep it in mind if you plan to grow plants that don't like sitting in wet soil. But with precision in your watering skills, you can avoid all the problems that accompany the lack of proper drainage in a terrarium.

Living Art Garden

Living art is an enchanting way to display succulent plants. You can get a bunch of pre-made frames just for gardening. Then, all you have to do is fill the frames with plants of your choosing.

Alternatively, consider building your customized living frame with the perfect design, shape, and size. If you are handy with carpentry tools or know someone, try building a deep wooden box.

Then, cover this box with wire screens and attach the picture frame you purchased. Finally, fill the box with soil and peat moss, then put your succulents inside the wireframe. Use various species to create a bright and colorful tapestry of different sizes, textures, and shapes.

Windowsill Herb Garden

The best place for this garden design is your kitchen because that's where it is most functional. Growing a kitchen garden with many of your favorite herbs is a beautiful thing. The mere sight of the varying herbs lining your windowsill is delightful, especially because you know they are only an arm's length away when you need them. With adequate sunlight and window space, you might even be able to grow more than herbs; think tomatoes and chili peppers for your windowsill garden.

A few beautiful pots, containers, or jars are enough to light up the kitchen.

Hanging Baskets

If you don't want plants on your floors and counters, hanging baskets are one of the best ways to display your plants in an indoor garden. They complement an established garden excellently. The presence of nature in your home gives an incredibly refreshing feeling.

Ensure you choose baskets without drainage holes. If they do have holes, consider getting drainage plugs to keep the water from the soil from messing up your floors. You can hang basic planters, macramé hangers, and even glass terrariums. Keep the gardening pots stylish, though.

Matching Pots

Have you ever seen a garden where the grower has all their plants in matching pots? Whether it is terracotta, plain white, or pots with an arrangement of colors, planting in matching pots is a lovely design for an indoor garden.

Select a set of plain or terracotta pots with the same design and varying sizes to create a visually aesthetic theme throughout your grow room. You could try different styles with a uniform color or different colors with a uniform style. Remember to keep the plants in the correct proximity to one another regarding space and light requirements.

This will give your indoor garden a single unifying element and create an elegant display around your home.

Balcony Garden

Suppose you have a balcony in your home; you can grow a variety of vegetables with such little space. Tomatoes, spinach, and lettuce are some of the best crops to grow in pots on your balcony or patio.

Cucumbers, squash, and carrots also thrive well in environments like that. They are considered a new gardener's best friend because of how easy they are to grow anywhere.

You can add several other designs to your indoor garden, but for now, these are the most straightforward ideas to start with.

Below are some tips to help you pick the perfect design for you:

> • Stick with the first design you choose. Settling for one design amidst the array of available ones can be quite challenging. And that is why you should pick any design and stick with it. (If you don't, you might never make up your mind!) Consider the exact theme you want before choosing any design, and be sure it fits your home's look.

> • Apply the "less is more" concept. You need not grow as many plants as possible just to utilize every available space indoors. That might leave your plants squished and struggling to stay alive. Remember that they need space to breathe.

> • Be certain that you have total control over the space where your grow room will be. Avoid spaces where factors you can't control can affect your plants. This will help you gain complete control over the amount of light, air, water, and TLC that your plants get.

Indoor gardens provide you an opportunity to be as stylish as you want with your gardening. It's all up to you to choose the perfect system and design that suit your home and lifestyle as best as possible. Keep everything discussed in this chapter in mind when choosing the right design for your successful garden.

Chapter Four: Supplies for Indoor Gardening

To build a successful indoor garden, you need the right gardening supplies; they make your work easier. Regardless of how small or big you want your grow room to be, you'll want to create a checklist of everything you need.

Before you get supplies, determine the exact kinds of vegetables, fruits, flowers, and herbs you want to grow. This is very important as it will influence your choice of supplies.

Establishing what you'd like to grow and where you'd like to grow them will determine the type of soil, pots, lighting, etc., to purchase. Read to the end to know the recommended plants and make your selection before writing a shopping list.

Also, you need to decide if you will grow your plants from seedlings, cuttings, or adults. Young plants have different needs from full-grown plants. And this can affect the fertilizer and lighting requirements.

You need a handful of specific tools to make your indoor garden a success. Despite what many people think or assume, the tools for indoor and outdoor gardening are quite different. When you think of gardening tools, the first things that come to mind are probably rakes, spades, shovels, cultivators, etc. None of these are meant for indoor gardening.

Gardening supplies can be categorized into essentials and non-essentials. The essentials are supplies you can't do without, needing them to operate and maintain a functional garden. Non-essentials, on the other hand, are supplies that can make your work easier but aren't exactly compulsory to have. You can run a garden fine without the non-essential supplies.

Here are the essential supplies and tools you need to get your indoor garden running.

Pots and Containers

Pots containing potting soil

Once you decide on what to grow, you will know just how much space the roots need. Also, you can determine how big the plants might get. Don't forget that some of the plants you select might need re-potting if the roots become too large for their current containers. Some, in comparison, don't mind staying in smaller pots.

Pots and containers for your plants are some of the basic supplies to get for an indoor garden. Still, you can't just go into your local store to purchase any pot or container you see. Size is vital when selecting pots for your garden.

If a pot is too small, it can stunt your plants' growth. If it's too large, it can obstruct proper drainage and cause your roots to rot. Therefore, you need to know your plants' specific potting needs to find the right-sized pots.

Some other things to consider when buying containers are the material and drainage efficiency. Pots and containers made from upcycled and absorbent materials tend not to hold moisture as efficiently as your roots may need; you'll find yourself watering the plants more frequently. If you are a busy person, this might seem like a hassle and tempt you to neglect your plants.

Plastic and metal containers hold water more efficiently, and they depend on drainage holes to get rid of excess moisture. For new indoor gardeners, drainage holes are important in containers because they serve as a fail-safe for over-watering.

Potting Soil

Unless you want to use a hydroponic gardening system, the soil is one of the basic supplies to get for your indoor garden. But here's the catch: you must get the right type of soil. New gardeners rarely know the difference between topsoil and potting soil. They believe you can use any type of "dirt" for planting.

While topsoil is best for outdoor gardening, it won't drain properly in an enclosed space. Therefore, it is not right for an indoor garden. Potting soil allows for proper drainage since it was made to be fluffier.

If possible, tailor your potting soil according to the specific plant you are growing. Succulents, cactus, and rosemary, for instance, grow well in rough, well-drained soil that contains one-third of sand. Seedlings are best grown in light and soilless mix since that is more moisture-retentive.

A good potting soil consists of perlite, vermiculite, and peat moss. These are soil-less mixes that are moisture-absorbent and compaction-resistant. Still, they are inclined to dry out faster than other potting mixes.

Since they rarely contain nutrients of any kind, you must provide your plants with a regular fertilizer supply. On the other hand, a soil-less mix is great for indoor plants because it is sterile, which means the possibility of introducing pests or diseases is limited.

You might want to add organic matters such as compost peat, leaf mold, finished compost, and garden soil to your indoor potting mix. This is because any growing medium that contains up to 20 percent organic components is less likely to dry out as quickly as a soilless mix. This enables you to add nutrients and beneficial microorganisms to the mix.

When purchasing a potting mix, the most important thing is to ensure that the texture is light enough to make room for water, air, and healthy root growth. Heavier potting mixes are best used for plants that will be in direct contact with sunlight. They won't dry out as fast. Lighter soil mixes are for crops that require little water for root growth.

Some plants need fertilizers once they are in the active stages of the growth cycle. Sometimes, the soil's nutrients become depleted. Other times, the potting mix simply has a low soil ratio. In any of these cases, a fertilizer will come in handy. So, consider adding fertilizer to your shopping list for indoor garden supplies.

You'd need an outdoor garden fertilizer for your indoor plants, so you have to follow the instructions highlighted for indoor plants. You might need to reduce the use to about one-fourth.

Remember that plants in hydroponic gardens rely on liquid nutrient solutions because they need not absorb nutrients from the soil. That means you don't need to purchase soil or fertilizer if you plan to own a water-based garden.

Watering System

Water is essential for plants, and you need to know how much water your garden will be needing; it's imperative for the survival of your crops. Some plants enjoy a downpour of water. Some don't want you to get their leaves wet at all. Some prefer a mild shower, and others just need you to water their bottoms.

You can water your plants with just about anything, but you might want to get watering cans that are designed to mist plants in precise ways. For example, any watering can with an elongated spout gets water below the leaves and directly into the soil. Using a cup, bucket, or jug can cause an overflow of water which can cause root stress.

Plants that enjoy getting a light shower are best watered with a misting bottle or a sprinkler attachment. A drip tray might be essential if your containers have drainage holes. Deep watering means you need larger drip trays.

A larger drip tray is ideal for plants that enjoy bottom watering. Just fill the tray with water and leave the roots to absorb most of it. Bottom watering can also be done with a large container where you can submerge your pot until the root soaks up all the water it needs.

In case you settle for hydroponic gardening, the containment setup will also serve as the watering system. Hydroponic systems naturally come with a water reservoir that must be refilled at intervals, depending on the plants you grow.

Many gardeners like this system combine most of the tools required for gardening into a single efficient gardening system.

Grow Lights

Some houseplants require long hours of direct sunlight season round, while others survive on low light. As you've learned, a south-facing window can provide ample sunlight for the sun-loving plants. However, natural light is not always sufficient for an indoor garden. To grow high-light and medium-light plants with minimal natural light, you must get grow lights.

Grow lights allow you to grow as many varieties of plants as you want without worrying about lighting. You can grow houseplants, vegetables, fruits, flowers, and orchids with a grow light set. They are ideal for starting seeds because they ensure that you get stocky, green seedlings.

You can grow herbs and greens under light with as minimal natural light as possible. But to choose the right light system for your plants, you need to learn how plants use light. Refer to chapter two on how light helps plants.

When purchasing a grow light system, you must consider a few things. Sunlight works perfectly for plant growth because it contains the complete light spectrum and rainbow colors.

So, to grow plants indoors, you need a light system that offers the full spectrum, like the sun. A full-spectrum bulb replicates the natural sun spectrum by producing a blend of cool and warm lights. This makes them excellent for growing herbs, houseplants, and other crops.

Fluorescent and LED lights both produce full-spectrum light. However, LED lights are much better for the growing environment. Plus, they make less dent in your wallet.

The brightness of a grow light determines the intensity of light received by plants. The plant's closeness to the light source also affects this. Plants' need for light intensity differs according to their species and natural growing environments.

For instance, plants native to sunny climates require more sunlight than plants that evolved in shady forests and tropical jungles. Some houseplants are comfortable being 10 inches away from any light source. If you have foliage plants, they prefer being as far away as possible from a light source. Experts recommend 35 to 36 inches distance.

On the other hand, flowering plants such as orchids, citrus, gardenias, and many vegetable plants need to be as close as possible to the light source. This is because they require a higher intensity for flowering and fruit production.

Another thing to consider with the lighting system is the duration. Regardless of the types of plants in your grow room, they need a rest from light. Plants respire in the dark as part of their growth process.

The duration between active growth time and rest time is key to varying biological processes, such as the fruit and bud setting and the growth rate. Getting a light system with an inbuilt timer enables you to set the preferred duration.

According to their preferred light duration, botanists categorize plants into Short-day plants, Long-day plants, and Day-neutral plants.

Short-day plants need less than 12 hours of daily light to thrive. Before they set buds and flowers, they might even require a series of shorter days. Long-day plants need up to 18 hours of light per day. Most garden flowers and vegetables are long-day plants. They become pale and spindly when they don't get enough light. Day-neutral plants will thrive as long as they receive 8 to 12 hours of light all season.

Grow lights come in different spectrums, sizes, and shapes, so you are sure to find one that fits your budget and plants. There are many cheap lights available if you just need something to give a boost, no matter how little, to your plants.

PH Meter/Soil Test Kit

A PH meter is a necessity in any garden. Whether you are growing with soil or hydroponics, you need it for your nutrient-feeding schedule. You can't afford to feed your plants with nutrients with an unbalanced PH. That mistake can cause nutrient deficiencies and burn. It can also restrict your plants' nutrient uptake.

Of course, you could try measuring the pH of the nutrient yourself. But using a PH test kit or meter can help ensure you never doubt your measurements. It will assist in determining PH levels so you don't end up killing your plants.

Humidifier

It's been established that houseplants need high humidity levels to thrive in an indoor environment. Depending on the area you live in, a humidifier can be an essential supply or not. You can provide your plants with humidity in different ways.

In an earlier chapter, you learned tips that can help increase the humidity in your home for your plants' growth. But consider getting an actual humidifier if these tips aren't enough.

There are three types of humidifiers you can get. They are:

- **Warm mist humidifiers:** These are what most gardeners are familiar with. They work in a straightforward way. You can use them to heat water as high as you want until it becomes water vapor. The vapor is then released to the immediate environment to increase the humidity levels.

- **Evaporative humidifiers**: These are not as common as the former. Unlike warm mist humidifiers, evaporative humidifiers create vapor from airflow. They work like swamp coolers. They draw water from their reservoir through a wicking material which a fan blows air over, thereby adding water vapor to the air. This then flows out into the grow room, providing your plants with the humidity they need.

- **Cold-mist humidifiers**: These utilize less energy. You can also run them for extended periods, making them an ideal choice if you want low maintenance.

You are likely wondering whether the type of mist (cold or warm) your humidifier puts out matters. No, it doesn't. The drop or rise in temperature resulting from the cold or warm mist from the humidifier barely affects anything.

It's up to you to decide if you want a cold-mist or a warm-mist humidifier. The key difference is that warm-mist humidifiers create mist through evaporation, which purifies the water vapor. But they also use a lot of electricity since they heat the water first.

Here's what to look for when purchasing the right humidifier for your indoor plants:

- **Design**: The design of your humidifier should be as simple as possible because you would be using it most of the time. That means it should be easy to take apart and maintain.

- **Run time**: Ideally, the humidifier should have a run time of 12 to 24 hours. You don't want one you have to refill constantly.

Also, make sure the humidifier is small and handy to ensure ease of use.

Hand Fork

Remember that indoor plants have limited access to soil nutrients compared to outdoor plants. Therefore, to keep them healthy, you need to add fertilizer and compost or peat moss to the containers. It's difficult to do this effectively without a hand fork, and that makes it a must-have tool.

A hand fork typically features at least three prongs to help planters work the soil, aerate it, and ensure that nutrients are evenly distributed in the container or pot. You can also use it for planting and transplanting.

Pruners

Pruners are an essential tool no indoor gardener wants to skimp on. You need a well-designed set of pruners to snip stems and leaves. They help manage unwanted growth with precision. However, poor quality pruners can snip off a plant's foliage, which could crush and tear the stems.

That, in turn, leaves the plants vulnerable to infestation and diseases. So, make sure that the blades of your pruners are sharp and of quality. Replace your pruners when the blades start to get blunt.

Keep the blades sharp, clean, and free from disease by wiping them with rubbing alcohol after every use. That will help prevent bluntness and unnecessary damage to your plants.

Plant Sensor

This isn't a necessary tool to have, but it can be incredibly helpful if you don't have much of a green thumb, i.e., you have a plant-killing tendency. It is handy because it lets you know vital facts about your garden and the plants, such as the type, the temperature, and the humidity levels.

The Wi-Fi plant sensor can even send you mobile alerts to check in with the amount of light and temperature that the garden needs and feeding guidelines. If you are familiar with plant care, you don't need the sensor.

But if you've tried your hand at gardening in the past and can't seem to keep your plants alive, then you'll likely find the alerts and guidance from the sensor beneficial. So, if you don't mind spending the money, try to get one.

Neem Oil

Neem oil is an amazing oil for repelling pests and eliminating an infestation. You can add a few drops to the water before misting your plants, or just store it away for whenever you get a bug problem in your garden.

This impressive oil provides you with an organic means of combating plant pests without harming your plants. If you have a pest problem, it will kill the harmful insects and leave the beneficial ones alone. You can use it in an indoor and outdoor garden.

Heat Mats

You already know that your indoor plants require heat to grow. Of course, it's normal for temperatures to plummet during the winter months, but that doesn't mean that your plants shouldn't get the much-needed warmth.

Heat mats help protect your plants against the drastic temperature drop by heating them from below. You just need to place the containers on the heat mat to prevent your plants from getting cold feet and becoming dormant.

Of course, this is also achievable using a grow light beaming down with sufficient heat on the plants. But there's nothing wrong with having both grow lights and heat mats.

Pot Base

Containers for soil-based plants typically have holes at the bottom to encourage drainage and prevent waterlogging. You can collect the drained water and any soil that leaks through the base holes with a pot base.

That means you can easily collect the pot base and get rid of the water whenever you need to. It also means you can reuse it and clean leaked soil more easily. These are ideal for keeping your plants and garden from becoming a dirty mess. After all, you need the display to stay aesthetically appealing.

If you plan to grow a lot of plants, getting multiple packs of pot bases is cheaper. But if you plan to grow a quite heavy indoor plant that can only sit on the floor, it's better to use a rolling caddy that comes with a drip tray.

Rubbing Alcohol/Cotton Swabs

This is one supply that every gardener must have on hand. It is a be-prepared essential for when your plants get a mealybug infestation. Mealybugs look like tiny cotton bits in plants, and you can find them on the root, stem, and leaves.

These cotton-like balls are slow-moving bugs. To get rid of them, simply dip some cotton swabs in rubbing alcohol and dab them directly onto the cotton bits on your plants. That will eliminate the ones visible to you. You can treat the ones you can't see by creating a solution of seven-parts water and one part rubbing alcohol. Put it in a spray bottle and mist your plants with it.

Plant Stands

There is a wide variety of plant stands for indoor gardening. Some are suitable for displaying single plants, while others are designed for collections of plants. You need not go to specialty plant stores to get the best stands.

Look online, and you will find a wide array of sturdy and quality plant stands in different e-commerce stores. Plant stands are ideal if you live in rented accommodation since you can't exactly install shelving systems or hanging hooks around a rented home.

With plant stands, you just need to set them up and start using them. They won't cause holes in the walls, which means no damage is caused to the interiors. That also means you won't have to worry about your landlord sending your deposit back.

Spray Bottle

Not all plants need a heavy downpour of water to grow well. Plenty of them just wants you to mist them occasionally, while others need daily misting. Well, you can't use a watering can for misting. It's much better to get a mister that is dedicated to your plants.

Getting three misters is the ideal thing to do if you really want to be dedicated to your plants. One mister can be for daily water use, another for fertilized water, and the last for chemicals-infused water.

Pebbles or Rocks

Remember we said there should always be drainage holes at the base of plant containers and pots? The problem with this is less about the extra moisture and more about the soil leakages.

One way around this problem is to place a broken clay piece from another pot over the drainage hole to ensure that only water is escaping. If you are extra careful and you don't have any broken plant pots, your alternative is to coat a layer of pebbles around the base of your pots. That will help keep the soil contained.

Another benefit of using pebbles is that they increase the humidity levels as the water evaporates from the holes. That can keep your temperature and humidity at beneficial levels for your plant growth.

Oscillating Fan

Air circulation makes indoor plants perform better. An oscillating fan can help increase the airflow in an indoor garden or grow room. Just ensure you don't use one that directs the air right on the plants. That isn't healthy and can stifle their growth.

That's about all the supplies you need to get your indoor garden running. They will also help with the maintenance.

For aqua and water-based plants, you will need three essential supplies:

- A water tank
- An air pump
- A pipe system

You will also need water-soluble fertilizer. Since that is the only way your plants will get the nutrients they need, ensure you get the highest quality fertilizers. You only need to feed them the nutrient solution once every 4 to 6 weeks when you change the water.

If you live in a hotter climate, you can increase that since some of the water in your hydroponic system may have evaporated. You only need a high-quality water-soluble fertilizer to feed your plants.

Finally, you'll need a water test kit to check the pH levels of your growing water. Ideally, it should be between 7.0 and 7.8, depending on the plants. In general, though, the pH levels should be neutral with neither too much alkaline nor acid.

Additionally, some water test kits can tell you the levels of calcium, chloride, magnesium, and sodium, and inform you of the presence of boron in the water. By purchasing a quality kit, you will learn when to swap the water for a fresh one so there are no harmful or toxic chemicals that can affect your plants' health.

The next chapter delves into something more practical than everything you've learned so far. Discover what it is by reading on!

Chapter Five: Building Container Beds for Beginners

For purchasing containers for your garden, the market is like a buffet. You have an endless selection to pick from. But this only applies if you would rather purchase planters than make them yourselves. If you plan to buy half-grown plants, it doesn't matter since those plants naturally come in containers.

The surest way to fall in love with your indoor garden is to pair the plants with planters that match your style. Now, you can either get these from plant stores or build them yourself. That's your choice to make.

To buy container beds, you just need to look out for a few things the size, drainage holes, and style. These things will also matter if you are building your container beds yourself.

The best thing you can do is make your own planters if regular planters don't meet your specific needs. Or you can recycle materials and objects in your home to make new planters. One thing about DIY planters is that they are relatively easy to make. As long as you follow the set of instructions in this chapter, you should have no challenges when building your garden container beds.

Making your planters is also cheaper. So, if you are gardening on a budget, consider building them on your own instead of buying fancy pots and containers from your local or online plant store. That money can be spent on other supplies that are just as important.

Planters can be made from any material or object. You only need to make sure the planter has enough space and good drainage and that the material used is food-safe. The larger a container is, the easier your plants will be to maintain.

A bigger container can hold more soil retain more moisture. In general, you shouldn't build container beds or planters below 12 inches across. Bigger is the better choice for growing vegetables, herbs, and flowers in containers.

Containers are typically made from ceramic, wood, plastic, metal, and fiberglass. Wooden planters can be made from scratch. But to make containers from the other materials, you might have to repurpose objects you already have at home.

Each container bed material has its pros and cons. Let's dive into these so you can decide on which ones you would rather have in your garden.

Wooden Planters

Wood is a great material for building planting pots and containers. You can choose a modern or traditional style and vary the sizes based on the plants you want to grow. Suppose you want a custom-made container that can fit a particular part of your home or match a specific color. In that case, wood is the cheapest and easiest option for you.

With the proper type of wood, the right construction, and adequate maintenance, wooden planting containers can last for several years. Different woods can be used to build planters.

Cedar is a long-lasting wood, but it can be relatively costly. Pine is cheap but may not last as long as you want unless you pressure-treat it with preservation chemicals. Redwood is similar to cedarwood in terms of properties but is more expensive.

Wooden containers are easy to construct because they require easy-to-find materials and tools. If you have storage boxes and wine boxes, you can repurpose them to use as planting containers. The fasteners used for wooden planters should be made of corrosion-resistant metals such as stainless steel.

The disadvantage of wooden containers is that they decay pretty fast if not properly cared for. To prevent rot, always remove the soil from pots you aren't using. Also, ensure you reseal them periodically to prolong the container's shelf life.

Here are tips for building wooden planters:

- If you have some available wooden dresser drawers in your home, those can serve as planting containers. Either separate the drawers for single planting or keep them all in the dresser and draw them out in a graduated sequence to form a beautiful vertical planter.

- Use heavy plastic or nylon materials to line the inside of the containers to last longer. Find plastic bags with bottom holes suitable for proper drainage. Potting soil will go into the bags, after which you can plant the herbs, vegetables, fruits, or flowers.

- Paint the container with bright colors of your choice to add a unifying theme to the garden.

- If you don't have dresser drawers, get wooden crates from a flea market or yard sale. But avoid old painted wood as the paint from those may contain lead, which can be harmful to you and your plants.

- To make the containers sturdier and long-lasting, attach pot feet to keep them elevated. This will make sure they aren't sitting directly on the ground.

- At the end of every growing season, clean out the container and reseal the inside wood. Since you can also plant during winter, just swap the pots for different seasons.

• Don't forget to re-pot when your plants get too big for their containers. Remember that space is key to their survival.

So, how can you build a wooden planter from scratch? Follow the set of instructions below.

Size the Wood

• First, you need to decide on how small or large you want the container to be. This decision should be made based on the number of plants you want in each planter. The size of the area where the planter will sit should also influence the decision. For this example, let's assume you are building a box 6 feet by 3 feet (182.8 by 91.4 cm).

• Purchase your untreated wood, which will work best for the DIY project. You can also use cedar. Both can stay strong against all the possible elements that the planter might be exposed to. For a 6x2 ft. container, consider getting a 14-foot board you can cut down to build the planter sides. Since you intend to use your planter on indoor surfaces such as your deck or patio, you will require one more piece to serve as the planter's base.

• Note: Do not get pressure-treated wood. This contains toxins and chemicals that can kill your plants and add arsenic to your vegetables. A safe alternative to untreated lumber is to use ACQ-treated ones; the process does not include toxic chemicals.

Cut the Wood

• After sizing the wood, you will need to cut it down to the desired sizes. Get a measuring tape to mark out all sides of the planter. Identify the places where you will cut by marking them with a pencil or pen.

- Use a basic hand saw or an electric one to cut the pieces according to size (two 3-foot boards and two 6-foot boards). Be careful to cut as straight as possible.

- If you don't have a saw or you don't want to make the cuts yourself, you can ask the staff where you purchased the lumber to cut it down according to the measurements you want. They may ask you to pay a small fee for this service, but some also cut planks down for free.

Attach the Plank Boards

- Drill pilot holes in the two shorter (3-foot) boards. These will ensure that the wood doesn't splinter when you attach the screws. You need not create pilot holes in the 6-foot planks. Simply drill three holes from the end edge of the shorter boards, with the middle hole in the center of the board width.

- Use galvanized screws or any other kind to fasten the boards tightly. Galvanized screws are recommended because they can withstand certain natural elements without rusting. Line up the boards in a way those with the pilot holes stand on the external corners. Then, use a drill to ensure that every screw goes through the designated hole into the adjoining plank. You may use a screwdriver instead of a drill or drill bit.

- Measure the length and width of the container's inside to ascertain the bottom's size. With whatever measurement you get, cut the bottom plank with your saw. Then, put it inside the box and use the drill and screws to adjoin it to the sides of the planter.

• Next, drill drainage holes in the base of the container. Turn over the wooden box and create at least four holes in the bottom. These holes are important because they protect your roots from getting soggy from excess water in the soil.

Note: If the box is larger than the average planter, add a few extra drainage holes.

Add Finishing Touches

• Line the inside of the planter with a layer of plastic bag or vinyl screen. As noted earlier, the purpose of this is to protect the wood from rot or decay. If you use a vinyl screen, cut it to the same size as the box you used for the container base. Lay it inside and attach it to the bottom with a few small nails. Don't forget to drill drainage holes in the screen parts that line up with the container's drainage holes.

• Smoothen the container by sanding the rough edges. Doing this will help achieve a finished look. Although it isn't compulsory to do, it helps if you will be painting your planters. Use a sander or sandpaper to smooth out the edges and corners. Remove any possible splinters by running the sander along the boards' sides.

• Prime, stain, or paint the planter's exterior. Use paint that matches your home décor or the theme you have in mind for your indoor garden. You can also stain the box to allow the wood's colors to shine through. If the box is made from cedar, you can leave it alone without painting or staining, as the wood is a beauty in itself.

Note: Do not treat the interior of your planters as the treatment may contaminate the potting soil, and as a result, your plants. Instead, line the box with holes-laden plastic or nylon to protect the lumber.

After you have created the wooden container box, you can add a thin gravel layer. Then, add the potting soil for planting. The gravel is there to help drain the box when necessary. Remember that the soil or compost used is determined by the types of vegetables, flowers, fruits, or herbs you intend to grow in the container bed.

There, you have a new wooden planting container in which to start growing your favorite indoor plants. As you can see, DIY wooden planters are easy and straightforward to construct.

Metal Planters

Metal containers can make an indoor garden look fabulous. From tin cans to modern steel boxes and feed troughs, you can achieve a wide range of looks and styles with metal planters. A file cabinet can be repurposed to become a container bed. Whether shiny, painted, or brushed, all kinds of metal surfaces can work for metal planting containers.

Many gardeners consider metals an unusual choice of planting material. Still, they can add a unique look to your indoor garden. Plus, they are great as accent pieces. Look in your home, and you will find many old metal objects waiting to be reused as metal planters.

Perhaps the best thing about metal planting containers is that they develop attractive worn patinas when you leave them in the weather. For example, a copper pot may add an attractive touch of green over time. That improves the attractiveness of the planter and your garden.

Although they will end up rusty or corroded, metal planters can last for several years before they give in to corrosion.

The one disadvantage is that metals tend to get hot during the summer months or generally under hotter temperatures. If you aren't careful, this can make your plants burn and dry out the moisture in your planting soil quite quickly.

Fortunately, indoor gardening offers a way around that. You can use metal containers in the shadiest locations. Use them for low-light plants since those require minimal direct contact with the sunlight.

Tips for using metal containers as planters:

- You can use metal items as cachepots by setting a fiber or plastic container inside the metal container.

- Create drainage holes in the bottom of the container with a can opener. Or you can pound the holes in with the help of a large nail or an awl. The more holes you put, the better.

- Find plant colanders, metal cans, old **BBQ** grills, and other cheap metal containers that can be used for growing single plants.

- Don't forget to line the metal container itself with plastic material. Ensure you cut some drainage holes into the plastic as well.

Plastic Planters

Plastic is a diverse material for making planting containers. Some plastics are high-end and attractive, while others are cheap and bare-looking. But it doesn't matter whether you decide on a quality decorative foam container or repurpose a pail you once used to keep things plastic planters are practical.

For gardeners on a budget, plastic containers make a perfect choice because they are the least costly material. They are also lightweight, so you don't have to worry about heavy lifting. Additionally, plastic is the most diverse material, meaning you have hundreds of styles and options to choose from when buying or repurposing your planting containers.

A disadvantage of growing with plastic containers is that some can leach toxic chemicals into your soil, especially if you leave them in direct contact with the sun. Before you buy or repurpose any plastic for growing your edibles, make sure it is food-safe.

Tips for creating plastic pots and containers:

- Find old plastic pots you no longer need and spray them with enamel to give them a brand-new look.
- Use old plastic pots as liners for metal and terracotta planters.
- Apply plastic polish on faded plastic pots to restore the shine and gloss.

You have a limitless range of options to choose from when making DIY planters and container beds. It all depends on how imaginative and creative you are. Don't underestimate the usefulness of ordinary objects around your house.

Many , from teacups to whiskey barrels, can all serve as containers for your plants. Ensure you make drainage holes in any material you use for your container bed and that the potting soil is mixed appropriately.

Remember that the smaller your container, the less soil mixture you can put it. Therefore, the soil moisture level must remain correct as you have little room for error.

Find beautiful images of wooden, metal, plastic, and other planters made from random objects around the house and make your pick.

Chapter Six: Choosing Vegetables for Indoor Gardens

There are different varieties and options to choose from when selecting vegetables for your indoor garden. Most vegetables are warm-season crops, so they are harder to grow during colder months. Winter leaves outdoor gardeners wishing they had fresh produce from the summer.

But when you have an indoor garden, you won't have to worry about not having fresh veggies and greens for your consumption. The good thing is that the process of growing vegetables indoors is more straightforward than you think.

No matter your reason for starting an indoor vegetable garden, you want to ensure that you have the best gardening experience. The only way you can do that is to choose vegetables proven to be suitable for indoor gardening.

Vegetable gardening shouldn't be a difficult task if you care for the plants the right way. Before you choose a specific crop, learn about the growing requirements. As long as you create the right environmental and growing conditions, you will have a bountiful garden filled with delectable home-grown veggies in little time.

The thing is, you can grow most vegetable varieties indoors as long as you meet the growing requirements. That is the only thing that could pose a challenge.

This chapter will detail the ten vegetables you can grow indoors – both their growing requirements and growing process. More examples of veggies suitable for an indoor environment will also be provided.

Before we get to it, know there are two main varieties of crops: heirloom and hybrid. The key difference is that you can save heirloom seeds from your veggies for the next planting season, but you can't do that with hybrid seeds. Heirloom crops pass on the exact features of each specific cultivar from season to season. So, if you save seeds from a plant this season, the seedling will have the same growth habit, size, flavor, and color in the following one.

Conversely, hybrids don't retain the characteristics of a parent plant because they comprise two or more cultivars. Therefore, the traits are typically mixed up.

Heirlooms tend to have superior size, color, flavor, and growth, which is why they are recommended for an indoor garden. To grow heirlooms, know that you can't save seeds from hybrid crops as those won't give you the same plant as the parent.

However, suppose you don't have plans of saving seeds from your harvest for the upcoming seasons. In that case, you can grow hybrid vegetables in your garden. Just make sure you grow them according to instructions.

Tomatoes, peppers, lettuces, peas, eggplants, beans, and other self-pollinators are some vegetables that can be used to save heirloom seeds because they replicate the same qualities as parent plants. To prevent cross-pollination and avoid having hybrids, you need to plant insect-pollinated heirloom veggies several feet away from one another.

So, what are the ten best vegetables to grow in your indoor garden? Check them out below.

Carrots

Carrots are reputably difficult to grow, especially in an outdoor garden. But most gardeners find them relatively easy to grow in containers. With the right conditions, you will love the result of your container vegetables.

Some varieties of carrots are best grown in fairly-sized containers. Still, if your planter is big enough, you can try growing some of the larger varieties. Just know that smaller types give you a much quicker harvest, and they are generally more fun to grow.

Containers are ideal for growing carrots because of potting soil's loose and loamy nature, which, as you already know, is what you use for indoor and container gardening. That kind of soil gives the carrots room to stretch out.

Radish-shaped carrots don't take up much container space, so consider growing these varieties. Still, there are others you can experiment with to see which one works better with your hands. Some include:

• Romeo is a fast-growing variety that is small and well-fitting for a container. It is round and about two diameter inches.

• Paris Market a small, round French variety you can harvest in 50-65 days. They are sweetest when they are no bigger than two diameter inches.

• Nantes are typically ready to harvest in a 75 days max. This variety is long but shouldn't be allowed to go beyond 7 inches before harvest. The ideal growing temperature is between 45°F and 75°F. It is great for new indoor gardeners.

Other carrot varieties to consider growing are Thumbelina, Danvers, Imperator, and Chantenay.

In an indoor garden, your carrots should be in a location where they can receive up to six hours of natural sunlight every day. Even when cloudy, they will benefit from any amount of sunlight they get.

Carrots do well in loose soil with enough room for drainage, so don't make the potting soil mixture hard. Get rid of all possible obstructions such as rocks, pebbles, gravels, glass, or any other thing that can cause your veggie to become stunted or deformed. The potting soil should be of the highest quality.

Consider purchasing potting soil made specifically for vegetables as they contain all the necessary nutrients and requirements. Plant your carrots a few weeks before the final frost. Although they are cool-season crops, young carrots don't do well in extreme frost. So, keep the temperature at the right level.

You can grow carrots in any container that is not less than 12 inches wide and deep. The deeper, the better because carrots need plenty of space for healthy growth.

Tips for planting carrots in containers:

- Fill your planting container with potting soil to around 3-4 inches from the top.
- Sprinkle the seeds all over the soil surface, then add more soil to cover.
- Water every three days to keep the soil moist. Do not let the soil dry out, but also avoid letting water sit in the planter.

Germination can take up to three weeks, so don't be in a hurry to see carrot leaves sprouting. When the seeds germinate, you will need to thin them to provide more space for your carrots. Get rid of the weaker and smaller ones to give space for the remaining carrots. There should be at least two inches of space around each carrot in your container.

Once you have the baby carrots, continue taking care of them until they start to pop out of the soil. To care for them, you need water and fertilizer. Feed them with a balanced organic foliar fertilizer every three weeks. Don't use too much manure or nitrogen-laden fertilizers because those can cause your carrots to deform.

Water according to the soil and environmental conditions. As noted, you should keep the soil moist enough without soaking. Soil dries out faster in containers, so stay on top of your soil condition.

Suppose you live in a dry climate. In that case, try using a self-watering container to plant your carrots. That will help keep the soil moist and healthy.

Carrots can be planted in companionship with these plants:

- Cherry tomato
- Lettuce
- Radish
- Chives

- Sage
- Rosemary

Don't plant them around potatoes, parsnip, and dill.

Tomatoes

Homegrown tomatoes are probably the best things ever. If you know someone with a passive dislike for tomatoes, all it takes is one homegrown tomato to make them change their tune. Nothing tastes as juicy as a red, ripe tomato fresh out of a garden.

Not only do tomatoes taste great, but they are quite straightforward to grow. Except for extreme frosting temperature, you can grow tomatoes in almost any condition. They don't require plenty of space, which makes them perfect for indoor gardening.

You also have various varieties to choose from, depending on your personal preferences and region's hardiness. Cherry, Roma, Beefsteak, Long Keepers, and Main Crop are some of the most common tomato varieties to select from.

- Cherry tomatoes are probably the easiest type to grow. They mature early, and children love them. They can be grown in any kind of indoor planter.

- Main Crop tomatoes are the most commonly grown variety in many home gardens. They produce a bountiful harvest during mid-season.

- Roma tomatoes are also called *plum tomatoes*. They are small and long and are generally grown for canning.

- The Beefsteak is a large variety of tomatoes, which is why it is called the "big daddy of tomatoes." It is great for sandwich making. However, it never really matures until the growing season is well underway.

Most orange and yellow tomatoes are called Long Keepers because they can be stored for many months in cool and dark areas.

Tomatoes follow two growth patterns: Determinate and Indeterminate. Determinate growth means that the plant will grow to a specified height and width, flower, and spend the rest of its time ripening. Varieties that follow the determinate growth pattern are the best options to grow in a planting container or pot.

Conversely, indeterminate growth means that the plant will keep growing all season until the frost comes, which is when it dies. Varieties that grow indeterminately never stop adding width and height, so they aren't ideal for indoor gardens.

The growing time should determine the tomato variety you grow. Some take as short as 50 days, while others like beefsteak take up to 90 days to produce fruits.

If you want tomatoes you can use for a sandwich, go for the beefsteak variety. Looking to make salsa or sauce? Use cherry or Roma tomato. Note that cherry isn't suitable for sandwiches.

Tips for planting tomatoes:

- Put the planter in a location where your tomatoes can receive over six hours of pure sunlight and up to eight hours of light in general.

- Make sure the soil is loamy and well-draining with a pH level of 6.0 to 6.8.
- Start seeds every two to three weeks to grow tomatoes all season round.
- The ideal indoor temperature for tomatoes is 65°F or more.
- Use 6-inch containers and plant them ¼ inches deep.

In the beginning, keep the growing pot in a warm location, such as the top of your refrigerator. Germination should occur in 5 to 10 days, after which you can move the container to a more brightly lit location, such as the south-facing window.

The warmer the temperature, the quicker the plant will flower. Warm temperature also promotes growth. Once the seedlings are at least 3 inches big, move them to a bigger container. Then, start fertilizing bi-monthly.

Some of the smaller varieties suitable for growing indoors include:

- Tiny Tim
- Red Robin
- Florida Petite
- Toy Boy

Consider the fruit type, size, growth rate, requirement, and ability to set fruit in a cooler climate before choosing any variety of tomatoes. Many gardeners find that Red Robin has the perfect characteristics for an indoor environment.

Squash

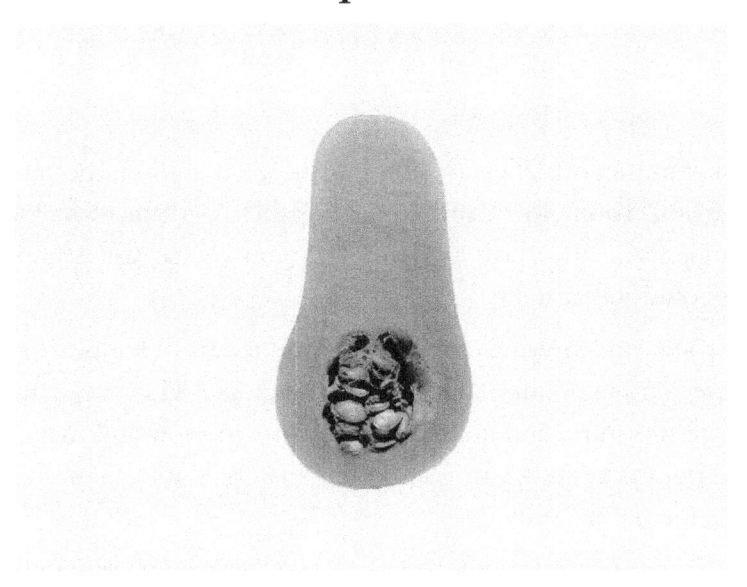

If you like squash, you may be worried that you can't grow them inside due to their large tendencies. Fortunately, there are varieties of squash perfect for indoor growing, so you don't have to fret about missing out on fresh squash supplies.

Several varieties of squash can be grown indoors. They are categorized into summer and winter crops. Most are vine plants, but there are a few bush varieties as well.

Summer varieties are large and bushy. They don't spread as vine squashes do. Some of the most common types are:

- Scallop
- Straight-neck
- Crooked-neck
- Zucchini

Winter squash varieties are vine plants, which means they will spread throughout your garden. They are categorized according to sizes, colors, and shapes. Some of the most common ones are:

- Acorn
- Spaghetti
- Hubbard
- Butternut

The summer varieties are the best to grow indoors because they require less room for growth, making them suitable for container gardening. Still, they give the same amount of harvest as those you grow in outdoor gardens.

Like any vine-growing crop, squash prefers warm temperature. Yet, they are hardier than cucumbers and melons. They need full sun, adequate moisture, and a fertile potting mix to grow and mature well. You should add sufficient composted materials into your soil when making the potting mix.

Both summer and winter squash are best grown in well-drained soil with high organic matter content. Add peat moss or compost into the soil to get the desired level of organic matter.

If you plant your squash seeds in a container around early July, it should take only 50 to 60 days before you have fresh squash to harvest.

Tips for growing squash in an indoor garden:

- Place a piece of fiberglass screen at the bottom of your planter. Ensure it covers the drainage holes to keep pests out and keep the soil in.
- Fill the planter with your potting mix until it's about 2 inches from the top.
- Put the squash seeds in the center of the container and add ½ inch of the potting mix to cover up.
- Water the soil until the drainage holes release excess water. Put the container in a location where your squash can get up to 8 hours of daily sunlight.

• Ten days after planting, when the squash germinates, thin the plants by cutting the weakest and smallest seedlings with scissors. Leave the two biggest seedlings.

• When the seedlings are 8 to 10 inches tall, cut the smaller of the remaining squash plants from the soil line.

• Fertilize your squash when it is around two weeks old. Then, wait until a week to harvest before you fertilize again.

• Water the plants any time the top layer of the soil feels dry. Regularly check for signs of pests or diseases.

To mix your potting soil for squash, use equal parts of compost, perlite, and sphagnum peat moss. Before mixing with the compost and perlite, moisten the peat moss to allow for easy combination.

Peppers

If you are looking to add bright colors to your garden, peppers make a great addition. From red to yellow, orange, green, and even purple, peppers have various colors that make them ideal for creating a colorful indoor garden. They come in varieties, from sweet to hot and spicy. Peppers are easy to grow, but temperature often poses the biggest challenge for many gardeners. It is probably the most important factor when growing peppers indoors.

Bell peppers are one of the most common varieties of peppers. You can produce regular bell pepper for your consumption with the right nutrients and growing environment. Below are tips for growing some inside your home:

• Mix coarse sand, vermiculite, and peat moss in equal parts to create your potting soil. For each container, make two gallons of potting mix. Add in two spoons of fertilizer with phosphorus, potassium, and nitrogen in a 10-10-10 ratio.

• Cut cloth in the shape of a circle. Make sure it is many inches longer than the bottom of your container. Place the cloth at the base and press the edges against the planter's sides.

• Pour your potting mix into the cloth until it is about one inch away from the top.

• Drop two seeds into the soil nearest to the center of the container with at least 3 inches gap between both. Use your finger to push the seeds deep into the soil until a thin soil layer submerges them.

• Dampen the soil with water, but be careful not to over-saturate it. Put the container in a location where the pepper seeds can receive natural sunlight throughout the whole day.

• Keep the temperature in the grow room between 65 and 75 degrees. Make this consistent.

• Water the soil regularly to prevent it from drying out. Once the seeds start flowering, use a water-soluble fertilizer to fertilize them every week. Again, the nitrogen, phosphorus, and potassium ratio should be 10-10-10.

• Look out for peppers to form. Wait until the peppers develop a sharp red hue over the entire surface before you harvest them.

Beets

Beets are the easiest vegetables to grow during the winter months, making them right for indoor gardening. As long as you keep the soil temperature above 40 degrees, you can supply your home with fresh beets year-round.

Naturally, beets have different varieties, from dark red and striped beets to sugar ones. No matter which ones you want to grow, a container is good enough to grow them indoors. Still, some varieties are much more adapted to indoor growing than others.

Some of the best beet varieties to grow indoors are:

• Cylindra has the shape of a carrot, contrary to the usual round look most beets have. This is an heirloom variety and is sometimes called the "butter slicer" or the

"Formanova." It takes just 60 days to grow and harvest. The Cylindra is a unique variety because it's cylinder-shaped, and that's where it got its name.

- Detroit Dark Red makes a colorful addition to any garden. By now, you should know the aesthetic and nutritional importance of adding a dash of color to your garden. If you don't know, the more colors you have, the more natural vitamins you will get from your plants. The Detroit dark red variety is a versatile beet type you can grow in varying temperatures and soil conditions. It also takes just 59 days to harvest.

- Chioggia is typically ready for harvest in 55 days. It is an Italian heirloom variety with an incredible flavor. It will make a great inclusion in your garden.

- Golden gets its name from its natural golden color, which differentiates it from other beet varieties. It can be grown and harvested within 55 days.

Other varieties include Mangold, Lutz Green Leaf, and Sugar Beets.

Tips for growing and caring for any variety of beets:

- First, beets are cold-weather crops. Therefore, they need a consistent soil temperature of 40°F. If the temperature is too hot, germination won't happen. If you live in a colder climate, you can plant beets all winter long. You can also plant it in the summer if you adjust your environment to match the growing requirements.

- Beets need loose, loamy, and well-draining soil to grow well. They also need part sun. The soil pH level should be between 6.0 and 7.0. Ensure there is sufficient compost in your potting mix before you plant beets.

- You can also use clay soil, but make sure you mix in lots of sand to improve the soil's texture and drainage.

- The first fourteen days after planting your beets, water them every day. Once the seeds start germinating, you only need to water the crop every 10 or 14 days. Insufficient watering can cause serious problems for your beets, so pay attention to the moisture level.

- Once the plants start sprouting, thin them out the same way you would your carrots. Keep the space between your beets 4 inches apart. Overcrowding can severely damage your harvest.

Cucumbers

Basically, there are two types of cucumbers, and both types come in different varieties. The first is the slicing cucumber, usually about 15 to 20 cm long, while the second is the pickling type. This one is shorter and never goes beyond 3 to 4 inches once fully mature.

Some cucumber varieties were bred to fruit even in an enclosed space since cross-pollination can't happen. Therefore, they are the best to grow in your indoor garden. Before you start planting cucumbers, though, there are some things to consider.

Forget about buying garden variety seeds because those won't grow well inside your home. Instead, settle for non-genetically modified (GMO) seeds because their seeds are more likely to germinate in an indoor garden.

Non-GMO seeds usually require more work in terms of pollination and pest/disease prevention. They also tend to produce fewer cucumbers compared to the seeds suitable for outdoor gardening. So, be sure you purchase seeds bred for indoor gardening.

The varieties of cucumbers for this purpose have flowers that pollinate themselves. They are disease-resistant and generally give a higher yield.

Bush cucumbers are varieties suitable for planting containers, as well as outdoor gardens. Some of the best ones include Bush Champion, Patio Pickler, and Bush Whopper.

Like squash, cucumbers are vine plants, so they need lots of space to grow well. If you are using a container, you need a big one to accommodate the large cucumber leaves. Otherwise, they will grow out of control.

Also, it's best to plant them with a vertical support structure such as a trellis to tell a major amount of the weight. Cucumbers like to sprawl and trail as they start growing. The tendrils are fast-growing, and they attach to anything within reach. So, be sure to pick a location with a lot of space.

Cucumbers need at least six hours of sunlight every day for optimal growth. Even then, you need sufficient light from additional grow lights if you want them to mature quickly. Without adequate sunlight, the cucumber plant's growth might be slow. This could lead limit your yield and cause the plant to produce smaller fruits.

You can purchase cucumber seeds the first time and then start saving seeds for the subsequent seasons from your previous plants.

Cucumbers grow well under a humid temperature, with loose, loamy soil and, as you've learned, plenty of sunlight and artificial light. The soil should have compost and fertilizer to give your cucumber plant the much-needed nutrients.

Before planting, get rid of all sticks, rocks, and debris from the soil. Then, mix enough organic matter and fertilizer into the potting mix.

Note that most cucumbers need a female and male flower to pollinate. The ones that don't are parthenocarpic, which means they can flower or set fruit without pollination. A good parthenocarpic variety that can be grown indoors is the Arkansas Little Leaf.

As the gardener, you can grow your cucumbers hydroponically or in soil. Most prefer to grow in water, however.

Tips for planting cucumbers indoors:

- Make your potting mix with equal part soil, compost, peat moss, and perlite, specific to the cucumber needs.

- Use a large ceramic or plastic container 12 inches wide and 8 inches deep, with plenty of drainage holes to get rid of excess water. As much as cucumbers like lots of water, they also like good drainage.

- Plant them around 2.5 cm deep. Once the plants start sprouting, think of the smallest and weakest ones as needed.

- Put your container in a location where the cucumbers can climb on a trellis or any other vertical support structure. That will lift the fruit off the soil and reduce the amount of space needed.

Following the tips above will ensure your garden has a neat appearance. Don't forget that the bush and compact varieties are the most suitable for growing containers and pots in enclosed spaces.

Lettuce

Lettuce is one vegetable you must have in your garden. It is a cheap way of keeping salad greens on your table. Lettuce is a cool-season veggie, so it grows better in a moist environment. This makes it perfect for a hydroponic system. But this doesn't mean that you can't plant it in soil.

Most lettuce varieties are better grown in cool conditions. Even if you live in a colder climate, you won't need to worry about the frost because the seedlings can tolerate it to an extent. Lettuces actually grow better at a temperature of 45 to 65°F.

For you to understand your lettuce's taste and flavor, they need to grow very quickly. So, before planting, you must have mixed the soil with organic compost and high-quality fertilizer to encourage rapid growth. The soil pH should be between 6.2 and 6.8.

Tips for growing lettuce indoors:

• Due to the seed's small size, sprinkle it on well-mixed soil in a plastic or wooden container. Then, lightly cover with a small layer of soil.

• Don't plant too deeply because the seeds require adequate sunlight to emerge from the soil.

• Mist the pot gently with the spray bottle to avoid displacing the newly planted seed with water.

• For optimal growth, give your lettuce up to 2 inches of water every week.

• Place the container around taller crops like tomatoes so they can provide the shade the lettuce needs. This will also help conserve space in an indoor garden.

Onions

Imagine having an indoor vegetable garden without onions. That's impossible, right? Onions are some of the best vegetables to cook with. You can use them on salads, and they add variety to different meals. Overall, they are just amazing.

So, you definitely should have some in your indoor garden. The great news is that onions are also eligible for your container gardening project.

Growing onions in containers is the same as growing them in the ground. The only difference is choosing the right container, depending on the number of onions you want. To get a decent yield, you need to plant several onions.

Therefore, attempting to grow them in smaller pots about 5 to 6 inches wide may be cumbersome for you. It is better to plant your onions in a wide-mouthed container at least 10 to 12 inches deep. It should also be several feet wide so you can have enough space to grow many onions that would be worth your time. Onions are also growable in tubs and buckets.

Regardless of the type of container you want to grow your onions in, location is the most important thing. Your onions should be in a part of the house where they can get up to seven hours of light per day. If you don't have an ideal location like that, ensure you supplement the natural sunlight with grow lights.

Water is key to onion growth, especially in a container and enclosed space. Onions need at least 3 inches of water every week. They might need more in hotter climates. Check them daily, and add some water whenever you notice that the topsoil is drying out.

If you plan to use a tub to grow your onions, the best part of your house to put that is the patio. That is where you can have the most fun by trying your hands at different varieties of onions.

Note that the more leaves you see at the top of the plant, the more inside the onion layers. What that means for you is that you have some big onions to harvest during harvesting time.

Some of the best varieties of onions to grow in an indoor garden are:

- Yellow Cipollini
- Ailsa Craig
- Red Baron
- Evergreen Bunching
- Valencia
- New York Early
- Walla Walla
- Gladstone

Best plants to surround onions with:
- Tomato
- Lettuce
- Chamomile
- Strawberry
- Rose

Don't surround your onions with beans, safe, garlic, peas, asparagus, leek, etc.

Spinach

Spinach is the perfect addition to your vegetable garden if you eat healthily and are gardening on a budget. You just need some affordable seeds, light, and a tiny space to start growing spinach.

In the past, it used to be known as the slimy, unattractive veggie that no kid likes. Nowadays, though, most of us know how delicious this green can be. Getting started with growing spinach is easy.

First, there are three major varieties: savoy, smooth, and semi-savoy. The smooth variety is sometimes called flat spinach. Newer varieties of spinach are constantly being developed to increase the growing season and improve the taste and flavor.

Savoy spinach is a sturdy variety with wrinkled and crinkled leaves all around. It has great cold tolerance. As you might have guessed, this variety is much harder to clean after harvest. Rather than wash yours under water, you are better off soaking them in cold water.

Hammerhead and Bloomsdale are the two most commonly known savoy spinaches. The former takes just 27 days to mature, while the latter takes 30 days. Hammerhead is mildew-resistant, and Bloomsdale has a knack for bolting rapidly.

Semi-savoy spinach is another cold-resistant, sturdy variety, but those are not its most notable features. It is more known for being disease-resistant and bolt-resistant compared to its savoy counterpart.

Semi-savoy is less wrinkled than savoy, which means cleaning the leaves is easier. However, the seeds mature a little slower than savoy seeds. Reflect, Tasman, Kolibri, Acadia, and Tundra are some of the most common semi-savoy varieties to plant in your indoor grow room.

The third main variety of spinach is the flat-leaf, similar to those you find in your local grocery. There are no crinkles and wrinkles on the left, so the leaves are easy to clean. This variety is also bolt-resistant.

Lizard, Seaside, Red Kitten, Woodpecker, and Flamingo are some of the most common flat-leaf spinach varieties. There are also some heat-resistant varieties, such as Malabar and New Zealand.

Compared to most vegetables, spinach offers a positively easy gardening experience.

Tips for growing spinach in a planting container inside your home:

- Use a container or pot 6 to 7 inches deep.

- Spinach needs full or partial sun, so place the pot in a windowsill location where it can get up to 5 hours of sunlight per day.

- The soil should have a pH level between 6.5 and 7.0 and should be well-draining. Naturally, add some compost and fertilizer to the potting mix in your container before planting. Spinach needs as many nutrients as possible.

- Water the seeds regularly to keep the soil moist until they start germinating. Be careful not to drench them. Always water whenever you feel the topsoil around them getting dry.

Of course, you should thin out the leaves to make more room for the spinach for growth and early maturation.

Radishes

To enjoy some harvest quickly, then consider planting some radish in your garden. This is a great veggie that does not take long to grow or harvest. They not only do well in small spaces, but they also have a great flavor. Nobody dislikes the crunchy taste of a freshly picked garden radish.

In fact, they are an excellent veggie for you to begin your gardening journey with. Plus, you can use them for training your kids on the joy of gardening. Children can grow radishes and start seeing the fruit of their hard work in as little as seven days.

There are more varieties of radishes than you can imagine. The best ones to consider for your garden are the Cherry Belle (also called Red Globes), White Icicle, Chinese Red Meat, Black Radish, White Radish, Daikon, Snowball, and French Breakfast.

Radishes can tolerate most temperature levels but may bolt to seed if the temp is too high. They also grow in different soils. But to get the best result, plant your radishes in a thoroughly composted potting mix. A mix of loamy and sandy soil is the best for this sweet veggie. Your soil should have a pH between 5.8 and 6.8.

The soil should be well-drained because radishes don't function well with wet feet. Add sufficient high-quality fertilizer to the mix before planting.

Radishes like plenty of sunlight, but they also like partial shade when the temp is too high. Plant them near taller veggies like tomatoes, beans, and peas. Find a sunny windowsill with afternoon shade for your radish container to sit.

Never grow them in the full shade because all their energy and nutrients will be expended towards leaf growth. Rotate the crops to prevent disease.

Besides the ten vegetables explained in-depth above, other veggies you can plant in an indoor garden are:

- Potatoes
- Cauliflower
- Garlic
- Broccoli
- Avocado
- Microgreens
- Mushrooms
- Dwarf Beans
- Scallions
- Eggplant
- English Peas
- Kale
- Swiss Chard
- Sprouts

- Arugula
- Parsley
- Parsnip

There are several others apart from these, but you can get started with some here and then move on to experimenting with other types and varieties.

Chapter Seven: Growing Herbs Indoors

Herbs are some of the easiest plants to grow indoors, as long as you know the right things to do. The key to building a successful indoor herb garden is to understand the growing requirements of the herbs you want and give them exactly what they need. It's simple and straightforward. Before discussing the exact herbs you can grow in your garden, there are some things to know about growing herbs.

The first is that herbs need very strong light. The more light you have in the growing environment, the more you will like the results of your herb plants. Many people don't know this, but the more intense light the herb garden gets, the stronger the flavors.

Growing your herbs under a very bright light gives them the best flavor possible. Besides that, you also know that light is crucial to plants' growth, and herbs are not excluded. In general, herbs need 6 to 8 hours of light directly from the sun.

So, always place your containers in a bright, sunny window or any other location that can be considered a sunroom. These are the ideal locations for growing herbs indoors. South-facing windows are the best overall choice. You can place a small table or bench in front of the window and then arrange your herb containers on it. Do this if your windowsill cannot comfortably accommodate the pots.

Suppose you don't have a sunroom or an ideally sunny location. In that case, you'd need additional artificial lights to supplement whatever natural sunlight your herbs get from their location. A simple led or fluorescent bulb from your local hardware store is all you need if you aren't growing more than one or two herb pots.

Ideally, the temperature for growing most herbs indoors is between 67 and 70 degrees, which is excellent for most home environments. If you, at any point, want to slow your herb plants' growth, you can reduce the temperature to 60 or 65 degrees. Some herbs want a dormant period.

Herbs also prefer a slow, thorough, and infrequent watering schedule. Always let the planters dry out between watering. Examine the soil with your fingers if it is at least 2 inches dry below the top, indicating a need for moisture. But this generally depends on the size of the pot.

Don't worry about the soul becoming too dry to where it harms your plants. Even when the topsoil dries out quickly, there is usually enough moisture at the middle and bottom of the soil.

Infrequent watering gets the roots to grow deeper in the search for water. It is one way of ensuring the plants have a healthy root system.

Also, don't water your herbs too quickly, as this can push water right through the planter and out the drainage holes before the soil can retain the moisture. So, always water your herbs slowly.

You need not water your herbs daily, but follow a regular schedule three times per week. Depending on your home's humidity level, this could even be two times weekly. Some situations that may cause your herbs to require daily watering are:

- Small planting container. If the roots are filling up the whole pot, you need to switch to a bigger pot.

- Low humidity levels in your home.

- High-temperature levels. Too much heat can make the pots dry out much quicker. Move the herbs back to a location with more shade if the current location is too runny for them.

It's best to grow each herb in an individual pot. Combining herbs in one big container isn't recommended for indoor gardening. However, you can do that in an aero garden or outside gardening environment.

Usually, it's harder to create the right growing environment for several herbs in one pot unless you have the perfect environmental conditions. Planting in separate containers is the key to getting the flexibility you need for an indoor herb garden.

Doing that allows you to meet each herb's needs individually. If you still want to plant some herbs together, you can get a multi-herb planter from a garden center around you. But that only works find temporarily. If you desire long-term success with your herb garden, the best thing you can do is provide each herb its own pot.

Now that you know the basics of indoor herb gardening, let's discuss the ten best herbs to include in your garden.

Basil

Basil is a favorite of many gardeners. It is a fan of warmth and full sun. So, place your basil pot in the sunniest location in your kitchen, with a temperature of up to 75 degrees. Basil is an annual plant, so don't sit its pot near drafty or cold windows. It will grow better in a southern-facing window.

This herb is most famous for making pesto sauce. Still, you can use it in tomato dishes, cheeses, and vegetables.

The Greek Miniature Basil is one variety you can grow indoors. It's a compact variety that grows around 6 inches tall. You can use it in the same recipes as the Sweet Basil variety. Another variety is the Spicy Globe Basil which grows up to 10 inches high under the right conditions.

You can also grow large basil varieties in your kitchen herb garden with little to no problem. But they may not attain their full height unless you use a large container and turn on supplemental grow lights. So, you need not worry about the basil taking over your home. Lemon Basil and Sweet Genovese Basil are two other varieties that grow perfectly in indoor growing conditions.

With sufficient lighting, you can harvest your basil in as little as six weeks. If you have many recipes to use the herb with, start as many plants as you can. You can grow them together in a single, huge container to save space.

Cilantro

You can either love or hate the taste of fresh cilantro. There are no in-betweens. This herb has a powerful aroma and a peppery zing that makes it great for spicy recipes. You can use cilantro on sauces, stir-fried dishes, and salsas. It is popular in Asian, Mexican, and Mediterranean recipes.

Almost all the varieties of cilantro are suitable for growing indoors. The Calypso cilantrois variety particularly grows up to 18 inches tall. Another variety to watch out for is the Santo. Both varieties are bolt-resistant, which means they will give you a longer yield before the seeds set.

Cilantro herb prefers full sun or mild shade, so the ideal location is an eastern or southern-facing window. Harvesting can start in as little as 3 to 4 weeks. Early harvest promotes bushier cilantro plants.

Chives

Chives is a popular perennial herb with which you are probably familiar. It is in the same family as onions. Chives grow in clumps of shallow stems that are meant to be divided every three years. The taste of chive and its compact nature is all the reason you need to add it to your herb garden!

The crunchy texture makes this herb excellent for instant use. They can be added to omelets, cheeses, and soups and used as toppings on baked potatoes. You can plant any chive variety indoors, but the two most popular ones are the Onion and Garlic Chives.

Chives should be placed in an area with partial shade or full sun, like the southern or eastern-facing window. Compared to most herbs, chives like having moist soil. They are usually not ready for harvest until about 90 days after starting seed.

Dill

Dill differs from the dill seeds used in pickling. And this distinction is made through its other name Dillweed. This herb has naturally feathery leaves that take the shape of small fans. It is used in sauces, cheeses, salads, mustard and can be combined with butter or lemon on potatoes and fishes. An excellent indoor variety of Dill weed is the Fern Leaf Dill, which grows 18 inches high.

Dill grows well in partial or full sun, so a southern-facing window is just right for it. If planting from seed, try fitting three seedlings in an 8 inches wide container to grow in small bunches. That will give you a bountiful harvest.

You can start harvesting your dill once it sprouts up to 5 true leaves.

Oregano

Oregano is an herb with mildly hairy grayish-green leaves in the shape of an oval. It has a bushy habit, and that means it is a good herb to grow indoors. This herb is a favorite in Greek and Italian cuisine, so you might want to plant some if you have some Italian recipes to try out. It can be used with garlic, lemon, and tomato-based dishes.

The Greek Oregano is the most known variety, and it grows 8 to 12 inches high under the right conditions. Like any herb, oregano enjoys direct sunlight. Place its pot in a sunny window for the best flavor and growth.

Starter plants give a much quicker harvest than seeds. So, reconsider starting oregano from seeds.

Mint

Everyone is familiar with mint, but not everyone knows it is an easy plant to grow indoors. Mint sprawls quickly, though, so always keep it in a separate planter to avoid overcrowding the remaining herbs in your kitchen.

You can use mint for various culinary purposes. It makes an excellent addition to beverages. It is also used in desserts, and most famously, in lamb with mint sauce. Overall, there is no reason you shouldn't have mint in your indoor herb garden.

Spearmint is the most popular variety of mint used for cooking, thanks to its clean minty taste. Other varieties to consider are Chocolate Mint and Peppermint.

Mint enjoys partial shade or the morning sun. An east-facing window is just perfect for growing your mint. The herb also prefers moister soil like the Oregano, so you need to water and spritz it more frequently than other herbs.

The easiest way to add mint to your garden is to buy the starter plants. It's better than trying to grow it from seed.

Parsley

Parsley needs a pot larger than most herb plants to grow well indoors. This is due to its elongated taproot. It is one of the three herbs that make up the Bouquet Garni. The other two are thyme and bay leaves.

Parsley's fresh, crispy taste makes it a favorite in almost any cuisine. Its leaves are used in different recipes. The stems can also add flavor to stocks.

The most popular variety is the Flat Leaf Parsley, which many gardeners agree has the best flavor. Curly parsley is also used in salads and as garnish. It has a nice flavor that is somewhat milder than the flat-leaf parsley. You can grow both in your garden, but make sure the flat-leaf variety gets the bigger container.

This herb grows well on a sunny windowsill, so place it in the East or south-facing window. It has a high tolerance for cooler temperatures and more moisture than most herbs. It is easy to start from seed, but germination can take 14 to 21 days on average.

Parsley germinates more quickly when you soak its seeds overnight. This is one trick that gardeners generally can't get enough of.

Sage

You cannot start an indoor herb garden without the herb called sage. It is a reputed member of the Salvia family that serves both culinary and ornamental purposes. Sage is popularly used as an ingredient in brown butter sauce. It also works in bread, cheeses, stuffing, and heavy meat and game.

Dwarf Garden Sage is an excellent variety for an indoor grow room. Its compact growth habit allows it to grow up to 10 inches high.

Sage likes full, bright sun. Therefore, only put it in a south-facing window. Note it is also a short-lived perennial, which means you will need to replace the seeds every couple of years.

Rosemary

Rosemary herb has a powerful, warm taste. It is a fragrant herb that can be added to any indoor garden. The key is to plant as little as possible to prevent rosemary from overpowering the more delicate herbs with its strong fragrance.

You can use rosemary when roasting and also with meats and vegetables. Most recipes require you to chop the leaves finely. But if you wish, you can use the whole sprig to impart the flavor into your dish and then remove it before serving your meal.

The most popular indoor variety is the Blue Boy Rosemary which has a compact habit. This variety grows up to 24 inches high and has a quite nice flavor.

Rosemary is a Mediterranean herb, meaning it wants full sun contact. Still, put it in a somewhat cooler location. Never allow the soil to dry out fully before you water it. Consider buying new plants instead of starting seeds to grow rosemary in your garden.

Thyme

Thyme is a must-have classic herb in any garden. Its low-growing, well-branching nature makes it grow equally well in outdoor and indoor gardens. You can add it to slow-steamed stews and soups and then remove it before serving. It goes perfectly with anything from meat to fish, poultry, and vegetable. It is an incredibly versatile herb plant.

By its nature, thyme is a compact herb, which means you can grow most varieties indoors. The Lemon thyme and English thyme varieties are the most commonly grown varieties indoors.

Thyme is easy to start from seed and relatively easy to care for. You can grow it in groups together in a single planter for a fuller and nicer effect. A 5-inch pot can accommodate five or more thyme seedlings.

Apart from these ten herbs, other varieties you can grow in your garden include:

- Lemongrass
- Garden Cress
- Catnip

- Lemon Balm
- Chervil
- Tarragon
- Bay Leaves

Mason jars are the perfect containers for creating a vertical herb garden in your kitchen. You can mark each herb jar with your label maker to make the herbs identifiable.

Chapter Eight: Selecting Flowers to Grow Indoors

Whether you want flowers in your garden for aesthetic, culinary, or fragrant purposes, there are several options to choose from. You can make your indoor garden a purely aesthetic one by growing flowering plants only. However, the beauty of an indoor garden is usually in its diversity. So, it's best to have a combination of veggies, herbs, fruits, and flowers indoors.

Flowering plants add a definitive color, vibrancy, and scents to your home, and that is why they deserve to be in your garden. If you are worried that flowers are much harder to grow than other plants, don't worry.

The flowering plants here are some of the easiest to grow, and they perform incredibly well indoors. Some of these are edible, while others are purely for decorative purposes. Not only can flowers brighten your home and your mood, but they also add flavor and color to your dishes.

Many can garnish salads, soups, and desserts due to their range of nutrients and vitamins. If you are making body care items, you can even use some of your homegrown flowers to do that. It is important to know edible flowers from non-edible ones. So, there will be a tag to help you differentiate.

Calendula (edible)

Calendula, also called Calendula officinalis, is a flowering plant with bright yellow, gold, and orange flowers. It has a peppery taste that is quite distinctive. Calendula is used to add color to dishes, specifically rice, instead of saffron.

This flower has a longer blooming season than many others, which means you can grow it during winter. The petals can be used to add a dashing brightness to your summer salads. Calendula flowers may also be used to make tea with mild antiseptic and astringent properties.

It can be used to treat ulcers, cramps, and other gastrointestinal problems. Try combining it with another herb or flower to achieve the desired tea taste.

African Violet (non-edible)

This is one of the most popular flowering plants that grow well in an indoor garden. The African violet produces very beautiful flowers in shades of purple, white, and red. They bloom year-round, which means they will keep your home looking attractive no matter what season it is.

This flowering houseplant may not be high-maintenance, but the small, leafy plants do better when you put them in pots that let them absorb water from the bottom. Therefore, you need a 5 to 6 inches pot to grow them until they are mature.

To encourage the healthy growth of your African violet, eliminate dead leaves regularly and swap the pot for a bigger one once the plant starts getting bigger. Finally, don't overwater them because that can make them spot and turn brown. In extreme cases, they may even die off.

One thing about African violets is that they usually die off without warning after blooming and flourishing in a garden for several years.

Chrysanthemums (edible)

Chrysanthemums, also called mums for short, have a spicy and pungent smell that stands out from other flowers. They come in a variety of colors with equally various flavors. The most common are reds, yellows, and whites.

This plant can be added to rice dishes, stir-fries, and salads and can also serve an aesthetic value in your home. Mums do well with lots of sunlight and will generally grow healthy in well-drained soil.

Scented Geraniums (non-edible)

Geraniums are fragrant flowers. Their spikes make them one of the best-looking flowering plants you will ever see in any garden. Scented geranium has natural scented foliage, which differentiates it from many other fragrant plants.

There are different colors and scents, so watch out for your favorite ones when purchasing geranium from a nursery around you. Also, remember that the cultivars rarely bloom. Geraniums are grown mostly for their fragrant leaves.

These plants love the sunlight. They won't mind if you drench them in sunlight for as long as possible. You can place a container in your room if you have a south or east-facing window. Remember that they need direct exposure to the sun to bloom and thrive, so don't compromise the location for anything.

Begonia (non-edible)

You have probably seen Begonia flowers somewhere outside your home. Still, they come in a wide range of varieties that make them excellent plants for an indoor garden. Under the proper conditions, these plants will bloom almost daily.

Begonia is best placed in a very bright area, but you shouldn't leave it near a window as the drafts can cause damage. The colorful leaves add a splash of beauty to any room they are in, even when it's not the blooming season.

Some of the best varieties to grow are the hairy-leaved, angel-wing, and wax-leaved varieties. These have adapted to indoor and container gardening quite effortlessly.

Hibiscus (edible)

Hibiscus tea is made from the lush hibiscus flower, which comes in a purple, blueish, and pink hue. It is a huge source of Vitamin C and a common ingredient in different herbal teas. Thanks to its anti-inflammatory properties, it can soothe coughs, aching limbs, and headaches. You can use hibiscus flowers to make syrup, jam, and tea.

Bromeliad (non-edible)

This flowering plant bears a striking resemblance to pineapples but isn't eligible to be added to your edible garden. The flowers are quirky, bright, and colorful. The plants are compact and can fit comfortably in a container.

You can recognize a bromeliad from its basal rosettes and showy flowers, which come in a colorful assortment of pink, yellow, red, and orange. Many of the bromeliad varieties are air plants due to their tropical nature.

Air plants get their moisture from the atmosphere, so humidity plays a very important role in the growth of bromeliad flowers. However, this doesn't mean you shouldn't water them regularly. Just ensure you spritz the water between their leaves when you do water them. That way, they can take their time to absorb the moisture.

Chenille (non-edible)

Chenille is also called the red-hot cattail plant due to its bright, fur-like flowers. It is both a fast grower and a long bloomer, so you can have it in your home for a long time while doing very little work. You can grow chenille in your home during the colder months.

This plant tends to become partially dormant in colder seasons, so you will need grow lights to ensure it keeps blooming. Mist it with water and keep the humidity levels high if you want them to remain moist and keep thriving.

Some other flowering plants that will make great inclusions in your indoor flower garden are:

- Christmas Cactus
- Violet
- Pansies
- Nasturtiums
- Orchids
- Lily of the Valley
- Gardenia

- Passionflower
- Indoor Citrus
- Tasmanian Blue Gum
- Hoya Plant
- Bee Balm
- Tuberose
- Sweet Osmanthus
- Orange Jasmine
- Angel's Trumpet
- Plumeria
- Cuban Oregano
- Myrtus
- Miniature Rose
- Jasmine
- Spider Lily

Depending on why you want flowers in your garden, you can plant two or more of these in your home.

Chapter Nine: Fruit Tree Options for Indoor Gardens

Why would anybody grow a fruit tree inside their home?

Well, why shouldn't they? If you have the available space, there is no reason you can't plant a fruit tree inside your home. There are many things to benefit from the clean air to the beautiful foliage. And more importantly, the fruits you won't have to buy from the grocery store.

The general belief about fruit trees is that they are impossible to grow indoors. After all, how could you hope to fit those tall and huge plants in your home? Contrary to popular belief, there are lots of fruit trees that are growable indoors.

Dwarf fruit tree varieties are made specifically for growing in containers inside the home. They are appealing, and they offer you a nice change from the usual philodendron and spider plant.

If you've never seen a dwarf fruit tree, they are grafted into a stock that enables them to stay small and compact. But some varieties can grow larger than is normal for an indoor garden. So, you must keep the size manageable with regular pruning.

These days, you can find dwarf fruit trees anywhere from your local nursery to garden centers. If you can't find the variety you want in your local store, you can find anyone you want on the Amazon online store. Most varieties you find will grow well in containers.

If you get the tree from your local nursery, make sure you repot it immediately, especially if the roots are cramped. There, gently prune the roots and loosen the soil before putting the tree in a new container. Use a pot that is slightly bigger than the original container.

If you purchase your tree online, it will likely come bare, meaning it won't be planted in soil. You will need to inspect the roots and prune the damaged parts before planting them in a container.

So, which fruit trees would be good to have in your indoor garden? Find out below.

Strawberries

Not everyone is familiar with the ease of growing strawberries indoors. They are some of the easiest fruits to grow inside your home because they need little sunlight. Plus, they have a compact size, so you can easily plant a bunch of them in one container and then place them on a windowsill with the least amount of direct sunlight.

The normal temperature in your home should be near the ideal temp for growing strawberries. Some varieties do well in hot temperatures as well. If your home tends to get frosty during a particular season, you will need to keep the temperature at the required level so your strawberries can survive and thrive.

The plants dry out quite quickly, so watch out for this. Check them every day and water or mist them according to their needs. Keep the humidity levels high so they can absorb moisture from around them.

Lemon

You may be surprised to learn that lemon is one of the easiest fruits to grow indoors, but that is a fact. Naturally, you can only grow a dwarf variety for your garden. Some of the more ideal options are Lisbon, Meyer, and Ponderosa lemon dwarf tree. Do not grow a standard lemon variety because, eventually, you won't be able to fit it in your home.

You shouldn't save seed to grow lemon as any seed from a shop is more than likely to be from a full-size tree. Plus, it sometimes takes up to 6 years for a seed-planted tree to start bearing fruits. If you have the patience, go for it! It's usually worth the wait.

But you are better off buying a dwarf variety that is already growing. Most experts recommend buying one that is two to three years old. These will grow and mature much faster, and you can start reaping the fruits of your labor.

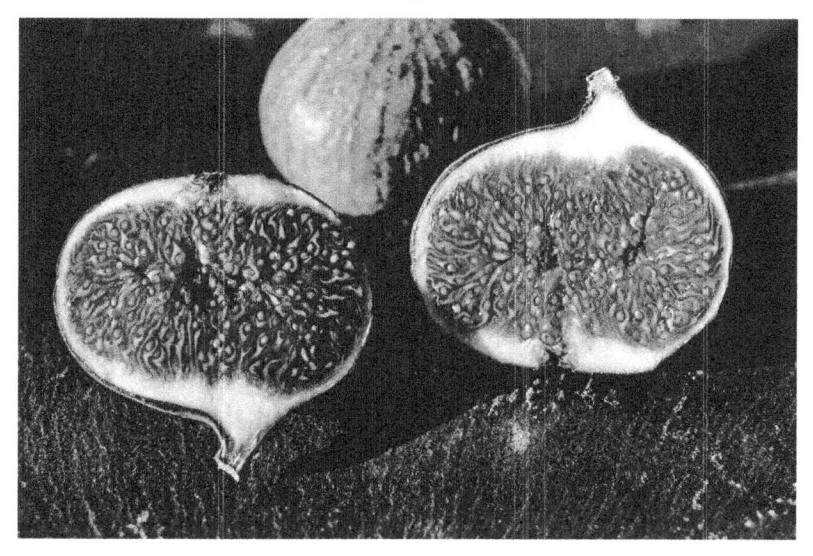

Figs

The best variety of figs to grow indoors is the Negro Largo. It performs well in an enclosed space. It does best well-lit location, but you have to shield it from direct sunlight. Temperature affects the size, so you need to keep it between 65 and 70 degrees to regulate your fully mature fig tree size. Most varieties only need you to feed them a few times during planting season.

Bananas

Like everyone else, you probably like bananas. They pump us with energy and are generally good for our health. In their natural habitat, bananas grow as tall as 30 feet. Fortunately, there are dwarf varieties that can be grown indoors. Add that to pruning, and you won't have to worry about a banana tree towering over you in your home.

You need only to purchase a sucker or corm from the plant store and plant it in a container filled with loamy soil. Then, place it in an area with at least 6 hours of daily sunlight. Water every three days and add some fertilizer once every week.

Some varieties to consider are the Super Dwarf Cavendish, Dwarf Lady Finger, Dwarf Jamaican, Dwarf Brazilian, etc.

Mulberry

A bush of mulberries is an excellent inclusion in any indoor fruit garden. In the wild, mulberry bushes can grow as tall as 10 feet. However, the dwarf version is usually between 4 to 5 feet, which means you can plant mulberry indoors.

The impressive thing about a mulberry bush is it can produce up to four harvests in a year, which means you are sure to get a sufficient number of mulberries to munch on! To grow and thrive, mulberries just need around 6 hours of partial sunlight. You can place the pot on a windowsill or in front of the window itself.

One problem to look out for is that mulberry bushes dry out very quickly. This can happen even more quickly in an enclosed environment. Therefore, you must regularly water your mulberry bush while also applying some much-needed fertilizer.

Other fruit trees you can grow indoors are:

- Lime
- Berries blueberry, blackberry, and raspberry
- Citrus
- Cucamelon

- Pineapple
- Orange

Many other fruits are growable inside, but you can begin your journey with some of these to build a diverse indoor garden within your home. Don't just stop at these veggies, fruits, flowers, and herbs discussed, though.

Research more about unusual varieties and choose those that seem like they will complement your garden well. Try new plants and varieties even if you are unfamiliar with them. That is the surest way to create the beautiful, diverse garden that is the dream of many growers. The good thing is that you can still do all these while gardening on a budget.

Chapter Ten: Getting Started on Your Indoor Garden

Now that you are familiar with the fundamentals of indoor gardening, let's move on to setting up your garden. This chapter will detail how you can plant and arrange your garden to produce the aesthetic result you want for your home.

Before you get to this part, you must have settled on a design. Decide if you want a vertical design, shelves, or other designs and styles explained in chapter three. Then, sketch out a rough portrait of how you want your home to look when you are finished planting and arranging your fruit trees, herbs, flowers, and veggies. Then you can start the practical side.

As a new gardener, try to keep things small. You might be tempted to go all out, but that can become overwhelming if you haven't tried gardening before. Try to grow one or two pots of fruits, herbs, flowers, and veggies, respectively, before you go all in.

Quickly, let's run through the things you need to do to get to this point again:

- Choose the perfect location. The most logical choice is inside and around your kitchen. The closer your herbs and veggies are as you cook, the likelier you will include them in your recipes. That also makes harvesting easier.

- Choose the plants. Select your favorite houseplants and purchase them from any local or online store. Select the ones you consume the most regularly. More importantly, make sure the plants you choose have similar growing requirements. That will make your job much easier, especially if you have limited space.

- Get the different containers required to grow the plants you want in your garden. Don't forget to get varying sizes based on the growing tendencies of the plants.

After choosing your plants, the next step is to plant the crops inside their designated containers. You have already learned how to create high-quality potting soil for your different plants. Follow the instructions on your seed packets to create the potting mix according to the requirements of each plant variety.

If you want an Instagram-worthy setting for your garden, remember that you can create that. Anyone can arrange their indoor space to look like something out of an interior décor magazine with the right tips and guidelines. Some things you need to set up the perfect plant-laden living space of your dream are texture, height, and layering. As long as you understand these three things and some general rules of thumb, you are good to go.

Indoor plants are generally more challenging to arrange to create a beautiful setting. Not all plants have similar requirements. For instance, you might think that two plants will look good together in the same area, only to discover that you can't grow them around each other.

Some plants look great in smaller, darker spaces, while others' beauty will only shine through if you put them in an open space. Therefore, you have to familiarize yourself with all these basics before you start arranging your plants.

Good arrangement does not only improve your interior appearance; it can also impact the health and growth of your house plants positively.

The first rule of thumb used in setting up an indoor garden is always to avoid grouping even-numbered plants together. Paired items give an awkwardly formal look, and you don't want that in your home.

A much better combination is achieved through a group of three, but you still need to ensure there is an odd number of plants in each grouping. Here are some things to note when creating a plant cluster:

- Do not put plants that are of uniform height in the same group. That will only blend them all together. Try putting one plant that is noticeably taller in the middle of each grouping.

- Find a commonality when grouping plants together. For example, you can arrange plants with dense leaves together. Color is another common feature you can use to arrange them. As long as every plant in a collection has one uniform trait, they won't look out of place next to each other.

Textures are another important thing to consider when creating visual interest. It does not just apply to furniture and décor, but plants as well. With the varying foliage textures, plants can help establish variation within a living space.

When arranging your indoor plants, you need to think in terms of contrasting textures. This means that you pair coarse with smooth, minimal with detailed, and so on.

If your home décor is minimalistic, you can go for plants with detailed appearances to complement the look of your home. If you have a textured home with blankets, layered rugs, and the likes, then you need plants with refined leaves in your home. That will balance things out for you.

You also need to learn to take advantage of your plants' height when arranging them. Try exploring the parts of your home at eye level or taller. While you can only display tall plants on ground level, smaller plants provide an opportunity to try out different heights.

Below are helpful tips to get your plants off the ground:

- Place trailing plants on shelves so their vines can grow out and give your indoor space an attractive jungle look.

- Put medium-sized plants too big for shelves and too small to serve as focal points on their own plant stand. That will make them stand out from others.

As you arrange those plants, check out the natural direction of their foliage. This is called the leading line, and you can take advantage of it to draw attention to specific parts of your home. Leading lines work better with plants whose leaves trail down or point upwards.

- The Zanzibar Gem and Snake Plant are two plants with leaves that go upwards. You can use them near your wall arts to call attention to them when they start pointing upwards.

- Plants from the philodendron or Pothos family's vines trail downward. You can display these in your bookshelves to draw attention to the fireplace.

Although it's tempting to match the color of your plant stands to your furniture and coffee table, you need not do that. Aspire to have some variation to create spice in your garden.

You can add color to your home without creating a rather dramatic or hodge-podge look by following the three rules of thumb explained above. Typically, you should have a primary, secondary, and accent color in the space.

Some ways you can achieve a more colorful look for your space include:

• Switching up the container colors. Don't just settle for a basic white or black color. Add more colors to your planters, even if it's a neutral one.

• Try different variegated plants so you can have some colorful leaves as well.

When designing, you need to remember your plants' needs. If you don't arrange the plants in a way that meets their basic needs, the entire space will eventually take on an ugly look. So, remember this as you set up and design your very own garden!

Chapter Eleven: Maintaining Your Indoor Garden

You must have picked up some plant care tips from every chapter so far in this book. But here, you will find an in-depth breakdown of the best practices for taking care of and maintaining an indoor garden while dealing with minimal problems.

Water

As established several chapters earlier, water is essential for taking care of your indoor plants. It is also crucial to the maintenance of your garden. The potting soil mix you use for planting should neither be dry nor wet. Instead, it should be kept moist at all times.

Of course, there are always exceptions to rules. Some thick-leafed plants perform their best when you let the potting mix dry out in between watering. If you keep the soil too damp or dry, their roots may begin to rot and subsequently lead to the dormancy or death of the plants.

You can tell when a plant needs watering by the texture of the soil. If it suddenly becomes cracked with a lighter color, that is a cry for moisture. After watering your plants, pick up the container and try to assess its weight.

After doing this a few times, you should be able to determine when your plant needs freshwater by picking up the container and gauging its weight. Of course, you can also stick your finger inside the soil to check the moisture below the surface level. It's better to use a handheld meter for larger plants.

Dehydration is a problem many plants often have to face because of neglectful owners. Never allow your plants to get to where the soil starts pulling from the container's edge, or the leaves start wilting. These are signs of dehydration, and they may indicate that your roots are already damaged.

Check out the signs below to know when your crops are under-watered:

- Transparent leaves
- Premature leaf or flower droppings
- Brown and curled leaves edges
- Delayed leaf growth

Overwatering is just as detrimental to plants as dehydration. It can force the air from your soil and open up the door for root-killing diseases to invade. In fact, some experts believe that overwatering is the leading houseplant killer.

Check out the signs below to determine if you are overwatering your plants:

- Both young and old leaves start falling off
- Mold forms on the soil surface
- Roots turn stinky and mushy beneath the soil

- Extra water standing at the base of the planting container
- Leaves develop brown decayed patches.

Suppose you lead a busy lifestyle, and you aren't sure you can keep up with the watering schedules of your plants. In that case, you can set up a self-watering device that will draw water from an available bowl into your plants' roots.

Room temp water from the tap is good enough for most indoor plants. It does not matter if there is fluoride or chlorine in the water. Plants generally love melted snow and rainwater. But don't use softened water too often as it may contain sodium.

You can water your plants from the bottom-up or top-down choose whatever watering style works best for you. Try to moisten your entire soil mass while keeping the foliage damp. There should be water dripping from the drainage holes drilled at the base of your planter.

Fertilizer

Fertilizing your plants is a huge part of the maintenance process. Every time you water a plant, it automatically leaks some nutrients from the soil. Even when that doesn't happen, plants deplete their nutrients reserve very quickly.

Unlike outdoor plants, houseplants don't have a stable source of nutrient replenishment. The only way they get that is when you feed them quality fertilizer. So, that is something you must do as regularly as required.

In general, you should fertilize your plants once every month once they start growing and flowering. Only withdraw fertilizer when a plant is dormant or growing really slow. If a certain plant shows signs of slow growth or yellow-green color, it might mean it needs more fertilizer.

But it could also mean that the plant needs less water or more light. Therefore, take your time to analyze your plants' conditions before you give them more fertilizer. Giving plant food to a plant that does not need it may just be worse than feeding it nothing.

There are different types of fertilizers but only use organic and specific to indoor plants. Synthetic fertilizers are more likely to burn your plants, so go for natural ones. Still, applying the exact amount required is very important.

Note that low-light plants won't require the same amount of fertilizer as the medium-light and high-light ones.

First, apply a quarter of the recommended amount of fertilizer on the seed packet label once a month. Then, watch out for changes in overall plant color. If it becomes lighter, start applying the fertilizer twice a month. Conversely, if the leaves become dark green and small with longer space between them, reduce the rate at which you apply fertilizer.

Note: Synthetic fertilizers build up soluble salt that can form a crusty pile of salts on your soil surface. Get rid of that layer and leach the soil with enough water every six weeks to prevent toxic salt buildup. Excess salt can make your plants susceptible to pest and disease attacks.

Repotting

Over time, some of your thriving plants might need a larger planter, especially if they grow the right way. Sometimes, you just need to change the potting mix for some fresh soil. The best time to repot plants is when they have just begun growing. Healthy and vibrant root growth means that your plants will adjust to their new containers very quickly.

Use a soilless medium designed specifically for indoor plants when it is time to re-pot. Then, make sure the new container is bigger than the previous one. The size difference should be minimal as a huge pot can cause wet feet and root rot.

Pruning and Harvesting

Naturally, you want to enjoy a bountiful and successful harvest after the growing season. While most people are consumed with ways to reduce maintenance and get more yield with less work, they often overlook one simple thing pruning. Some of the things that planters overlook are rewarding in ways that they rarely realize.

Pruning may seem counterintuitive to a successful harvest, but it is actually vital to the process. If you don't take pruning seriously, you may find that your harvest at the end of a growing season is nothing near what you wanted.

To clarify, pruning isn't the same as harvesting, even though both involve removing bits by bits of your plants. However, you can generally combine both for most plants. The main objective of pruning is to encourage plant growth, while harvesting is done to remove the parts that are ready to use. Some plants, such as ornamental flowers, need to be pruned even if you won't harvest them.

Pruning protects your plants' health and helps to control their shape and height for your convenience. When you remove a stem between two leaves in some plants, more stems grow in their place.

Rather than growing narrow and tall, plants need to grow outwards. You may prune your plants repeatedly for a contrasting reason. In a plant such as a tomato, you may have to remove the "suckers" to keep the plant straight and tidy. That will also keep them from bushing out.

By doing that, a plant can expend less of its energy on growth and more on fruiting. It also helps to keep some plants from breaking under their own weights.

How to tip plants successfully:

- Start pruning as early as possible so you can have a decent amount of produce in the long term.

- Do not prune over 1/3 of your plants. It's much harder for plants to sustain themselves when you've removed the bulk of their stems and leaves. So, you need to be as gentle as possible.

- Always wait until there are at least three sets of leaves on the stem before pruning any plant.

- Use a sharp pruner because blunt ones can cause damage and infection. Refer to chapter 4 to remember why you shouldn't use a dull or blunt pruner on your plants.

- Only remove stems that are above the leaves when pruning. That will ensure that the remaining attached buds have room to grow.

- For bushy plants, cut the top 2 to 3 inches of the stem. The plants will naturally grow new stems laterally.

- Follow an inwards and outwards pattern by removing any leaves blocking inner growth from receiving light and removing inner growth which isn't receiving light.

Harvesting is done when a plant is at its peak. You can tell this from the scent or flavor. Like pruning, you must be careful to remove as little of your plants as possible. Otherwise, the plants can't sustain themselves.

For example, lettuce is a hardy plant, which means you can harvest it in various ways. A common style is the "haircut" practice which involves snipping the leaves off at the very top of the plants. This technique is quicker for gardeners with plenty of plants to harvest.

Another technique is single leaf harvesting which involves removing the mature leaves and leaving the younger ones to grow further. This technique is great if you have few plants or just want to pick a couple of veggies for your salad.

The single leaf harvesting method can be used on lettuce, kale, arugula, and many other leafy ones.

These plants must be regularly harvested. Otherwise, they can become bitter. Some may even bolt without proper maintenance, and once bolting starts, the leaves become smaller and inedible. This means that the surest way to get a sustained harvest is to keep your veggies, herbs, fruits, and edible flowers trimmed.

Pests and Diseases

If you neglect your houseplants without inspecting and checking them out regularly, you leave them susceptible to pests and diseases. Not only can these affect your leaves and flowers, but they also damage the stems and roots. Therefore, prevention is much better than elimination.

The first step to avoiding pests and diseases in your indoor garden is to purchase clean and healthy seeds and plants. This very basic step reduces the risk of infection on new and existing plants.

If you aren't certain about the health of a particular plant, quarantine it from the garden and wait to see if there'd be any improvements. Doing the above is better than introducing a defective plant to your grow room, where it can infect other plants.

When watering your plants, inspect them and pinch off any dead flowers you see. If you notice a slight problem, treat it immediately to ensure it doesn't get out of hand. In addition, only use a healthy and clean potting mix. Do not keep cuttings off plants with questionable health.

Remember that many indoor plants will not grow to their full potential if you don't feed them regularly. Most gardeners never forget to water their plants, but many have trouble remembering to feed them with nutrients.

Plants become diseased when they don't get the nutrients they need. Plus, they have a better chance of fighting any disease or infestation when you regularly feed them a balanced nutritional diet. Be careful not to overfeed them as this can make the potting mix toxic, and that, in turn, kills the plants or slows down their growth considerably.

Here are some common plant problems that can cause pest and disease infestation.

- Variegated-leaved plants become green when you don't put them in an area with good lighting conditions. Flowering plants start losing their leaves when the soil is too dry, or the light level is insufficient.

- When in a draft, healthy leaves fall off the plants after first curling at the edges. A too-high temperature or too-dry soil can cause lower leaves to become brown and crispy.

- Flower buds fall off when lighting is insufficient or the air is too dry.

Some of the most common houseplant pests to watch out for are:

- Aphids: These pests cause stagnant growth and yellowish and distorted leaves. They also leave a sticky, black substance on your plants. They can cause and spread incurable viruses in your garden.

- Cyclamen mites: These can harm your strawberries, begonia flower, African violets, geranium, and other plants. The damage they cause is typically unnoticeable until the havoc is wrecked. They turn the leaves darker, curled, streaked, and distorted.

• Caterpillars: These typically affect certain vegetables and leaves. They eat holes in your leaves. You may not have to worry about them if they are only harmful.

• Earwigs: These garden pests have a frightening look, but they are generally harmless to people. Still, they can be a menace in the garden. They have a knack for chewing on vegetables, flowers, herbs, and other plants. You can identify an infestation of earwig by the holes and edges they leave on the petals and leaves.

• Mealybugs: The enclosed environment makes your indoor plants vulnerable to mealybugs. These are pests that leave a whitish cotton-resembling residue on the plants they attack. The cotton can be found on the leaves and stems.

• Scale insects: Scale pose a problem to any indoor plants. They suck the nutrients out of plants, leaving them susceptible to diseases. They thrive best in dry environments.

The most common diseases houseplants are prone to are:

- Leaf spot
- Root rot
- Botrytis
- Rust
- Blackleg
- Sooty mold
- Powdery mildew

Pest and disease infestation is not usually common in indoor gardens, but be on the lookout for any problem. You need not know plenty about the insects and diseases that can affect your plants. Just check out for them.

If you ever need to treat your plants, you can apply the chemicals in several ways. The most common technique is to dilute the insecticide in clean water and pour it inside your spray bottle. Then, you just need to spritz the garden. Dusting your plants with insecticide powder can also help eliminate pests. But this method may leave a messy residue of dirt on your plants.

Remember, caring for and maintaining your plants go well beyond watering and fertilizing them. Always be on the lookout for anything out of the ordinary. An early nip in the bud can save your plants and garden as a whole!

Conclusion

This book has explained many aspects of indoor gardening and the techniques that will succeed for you. But the fact, your success is more dependent on you than the techniques you've learned. Ultimately, you need to be willing to play around with a mix of veggies, fruits, flowers, and herbs.

Indoor Gardening is meant to be an introductory guide to gardening within your apartment or home, especially for those who haven't experimented with growing their crops before.

Over time, you will learn more about plants and gain more expertise as you try your hands at different varieties and systems. Gardening is not a one-system thing. You can continuously improve your knowledge and even come up with techniques on your own. Good luck!

Here's another book by Dion Rosser that you might like

References

Almanac, O. F. (n.d.). *Container Gardening with Vegetables*. Old Farmer's Almanac. https://www.almanac.com/content/container-gardening-vegetables

Container Gardening vegetables that grow in containers. (n.d.). Texas A&M AgriLife Extension Service. Retrieved from https://agrilifeextension.tamu.edu/solutions/container-gardening/

https://www.facebook.com/thespruceofficial. (2018). *Learn the Basics of Hydroponics: the Most Efficient Gardening Method*. The Spruce. https://www.thespruce.com/beginners-guide-to-hydroponics-1939215

https://www.facebook.com/thespruceofficial. (2019). *Here's How to Grow Delicious Veggies In Containers*. The Spruce. https://www.thespruce.com/vegetable-container-gardening-for-beginners-848161

5 Reasons You Should Start Indoor Gardening. (2019, December 17). Retrieved from Houseandhomestead.com website: https://houseandhomestead.com/5-reasons-you-should-start-indoor-gardening/,

10 indoor fruit trees you can grow at home year-round. (2021, January 11). Retrieved from Bobvila.com website: https://www.bobvila.com/slideshow/10-indoor-fruit-trees-you-can-grow-at-home-year-round-578652

12 best herbs to grow indoors. (2019, August 3). Retrieved from Balconygardenweb.com website: https://balconygardenweb.com/best-herbs-to-grow-indoors-indoor-herbs/

12 unique indoor plants with personality & traits. (2020, July 22). Retrieved from Balconygardenweb.com website: https://balconygardenweb.com/unique-indoor-plants-with-houseplant-traits/

Asthon, D. (2019, July 25). 21 awesome indoor garden ideas for wannabe gardeners in small spaces. Retrieved from Demiandashton.org website: https://demiandashton.org/indoor-garden-ideas/

Beginner's guide to indoor gardening. (2018, May 17). Retrieved from Backtotheroots.com website: https://blog.backtotheroots.com/2018/05/17/beginners-guide-to-indoor-gardening/

Carlson, R. E. (2019, September 30). 15 fun and easy indoor herb garden ideas. Retrieved from Homesteading.com website: https://homesteading.com/indoor-herb-garden-ideas/

Clark, J. (2019, June 10). 17 easiest vegetables to grow indoors for a harvest all year - . Retrieved from Tipsbulletin.com website: https://www.tipsbulletin.com/growing-vegetables-indoors/

Coelho, S. (2019, February 28). The beginner's guide to getting started with indoor gardening. Retrieved from Morningchores.com website: https://morningchores.com/indoor-gardening/

Courtney, P. (2020, August 9). 6 reasons to start growing an indoor garden. Retrieved from Optimisticmommy.com website: https://optimisticmommy.com/6-reasons-to-start-growing-an-indoor-garden/

Euan. (2020, April 15). 7 surprisingly easy fruits to grow indoors. Retrieved from Greenthumbplanet.com website: https://greenthumbplanet.com/easy-fruits-to-grow-indoors/

Fruits & Vegetables That Grow Well Indoors. (2012, November 12). Retrieved from Sfgate.com website: https://homeguides.sfgate.com/fruits-vegetables-grow-well-indoors-51958.html

Gomez, J. (2020, June 14). 20 best indoor flowering plants that are easy to grow indoors. Retrieved from Womenshealthmag.com website: https://www.womenshealthmag.com/life/g32843710/best-indoor-flowering-plants/

Indoor garden design ideas - 10 great options - indoor gardening. (2019, July 5). Retrieved from Indoorgardening.com website: https://indoorgardening.com/10-indoor-garden-design-ideas-to-inspire-you/

ION. (2015, March 30). 5 factors to consider to set up an indoor garden. Retrieved from Designlike.com website: https://designlike.com/5-factors-to-consider-to-set-up-an-indoor-garden/

Ionescu, F. (2020, May 6). 50 astonishing indoor garden ideas [with pictures] - YHMAG. Retrieved from Youhadmeatgardening.com website: https://youhadmeatgardening.com/indoor-garden-ideas/

Jones, N. (2019, November 25). 51 of the best indoor garden ideas for this year - A nest with A yard. Retrieved from Anestwithayard.com website: https://anestwithayard.com/indoor-garden-ideas

Lane, J. (2017, June 25). How to grow indoor fruits, vegetables & herbs. Retrieved from 104Homestead.com website: https://104homestead.com/how-to-grow-food-indoors/

Neveln, V. (2016, March 15). 22 of the most beautiful blooming houseplants you can grow. Retrieved from Bhg.com website: https://www.bhg.com/gardening/houseplants/projects/blooming-houseplants/

Peters, J., Garcia, I., & Morgan, B. (2018, January 24). 17 indoor herb gardens that will add New Life to your kitchen. Retrieved from Housebeautiful.com website: https://www.housebeautiful.com/lifestyle/gardening/g1877/indoor-herb-gardens/

Poindexter, J. (2017, January 31). 24 newbie-friendly vegetables you can easily grow indoors. Retrieved from Morningchores.com website: https://morningchores.com/growing-vegetable-indoors/

Postconsumers Content Team. (2014, May 27). 10 herbs and vegetables (and a fruit) that are easy to grow indoors. Retrieved from Postconsumers.com website: https://www.postconsumers.com/2014/05/27/grow-indoor-vegetables/

Rhoades, H. (2009, October 30). Houseplant maintenance: Basic tips for indoor houseplant care. Retrieved from Gardeningknowhow.com website: https://www.gardeningknowhow.com/houseplants/hpgen/basic-care-of-houseplants.htm

Sheehan, L. (2019, November 25). 15 rare and unusual houseplants to grow. Retrieved from Ruralsprout.com website: https://www.ruralsprout.com/unusual-houseplants/

Sood, G. (2019, April 11). Indoor vertical garden: How to grow & things to consider. Retrieved from Homecrux.com website: https://www.homecrux.com/indoor-vertical-garden/120830/

The Best Ways to Take Care of a Potted Herb Garden. (2012, April 28). Retrieved from Sfgate.com website: https://homeguides.sfgate.com/ways-care-potted-herb-garden-26463.html

The Editors. (2018, May 15). Spice up your dinner with these herbs you can grow indoors year-round. Retrieved from Goodhousekeeping.com website: https://www.goodhousekeeping.com/home/gardening/a20705923/indoor-herb-garden/

Trivedi, K. (2019, November 7). Gardening Tips: Indoor plants care and maintenance guidelines. Retrieved from Republic World website: https://www.republicworld.com/lifestyle/home/gardening-tips-indoor-plants-care-and-maintenance-guidelines.html

Wright, A. (n.d.). 15 perfect indoor garden design ideas for fresh houses. Retrieved from Sawhd.com website: https://sawhd.com/indoor-garden-design-for-easy-and-cheap-home-ideas/

(N.d.-a). Retrieved from Everydayhealth.com website: https://www.everydayhealth.com/healthy-home/reasons-to-start-a-garden.aspx, (N.d.-b). Retrieved from Well.org website: https://well.org/gardening/create-your-own-indoor-garden-guide/

Made in the USA
Coppell, TX
14 December 2021